Don't Bring Your Vibrator to Rehab

A Somewhat Comedic Memoir

Pam Gaslow

This book is dedicated to anyone who
has struggled with addiction.
Don't make excuses. Don't rationalize.
Don't waste your precious time on this earth.
Ask for help.

We finally came to the bottom. We did not have to be financially broke, although many of us were. But we were spiritually bankrupt. We had a soul-sickness, a revulsion against ourselves and against our way of living. Life had become impossible for us. We had to end it all or do something about it.

Am I glad I did something about it?

—*Twenty-Four Hours a Day*

Contents

RELAPSE

When I moved to Miami Beach in 2015 I was forty-five years old and sober. I hadn't had a drink in almost twenty years, and it had been eight years since I smoked pot. I moved to Miami not knowing anyone and not having a job. No one there seemed to work, or work too hard, so I fit right in.

I had recently shut down a children's clothing business I had run for ten years in New York and moved to Florida for a better quality of life. After I'd spent a couple months being bored and lonely (but warm), my friend Liz came to visit me for a weekend. On a Saturday afternoon at 4:30 p.m., after having disappeared for three hours under the guise of "going shopping," she called me from the bar across the street. She was drunk. She told me there was a hot guy there and that I should come over and meet him. I didn't trust her taste or her judgment, and I was pissed that she had been gone for so long, but I went across the street anyway. When I got to the bar there were only three people there: Liz and two other guys. Liz introduced me to one of them, Hunter, from four feet away, and I doubtfully glanced at him. He was wearing khaki shorts and a black T-shirt that said "Coconut King" on it.

I was wearing jean shorts and a white T-shirt that said "Depressed Hot Girl." His head was shaved, which I normally don't like but. . . "Come here," he summoned softly, as if he thought I was afraid of him. I walked over, and he put his arm around my waist and pulled me in close to him. He was extremely sexy with dirty blond scruff and blue eyes, and suddenly every tense muscle in my body collapsed. I was shocked at how turned on I was from just looking at him. He had this permanent devilish smile on his face. He was too much—too cute, too happy, too smooth. The type of guy you definitely need to use a condom with, at least the first two or three times.

Hunter asked for my number and, ten minutes later, while I was back at my apartment busy perusing his Facebook page, he texted me: "Hey cutie! It's Hunter from Purdy." Purdy is the name of the bar. Did he live there? Did it matter? Turned out he didn't live there; he lived in the building next door to mine. He also had two roommates and 3,834 Facebook friends and was fourteen years younger than me.

———————

Hunter's Facebook page is one gigantic red flag. It's an open book into his insanity. I mean life. His main photo shows him naked on his terrace, holding a coconut over each ball. Under "works at" it says he's a model/actor, although there is no evidence that he does either of those things professionally. I went through a bunch of his pictures and cross-referenced a few of the sluttier-looking girls. Then came the videos: 410 of them. I didn't watch all of them, but most ranged from him drinking to him throwing up to him swan diving off cliffs, skiing off cliffs, jumping naked into a pool, lighting his chest hair on fire, and worse. There was one of him running with the bulls in Texas, another one shows him drinking something on fire, called a flaming Lamborghini, and another where a friend staples his leg. And the only thing more entertaining than the videos and the hashtags (#finallymature—posted on his thirtieth birthday) were people's comments. Someone who looked older and wiser referred to him as "The Master of Disaster." Someone else wrote, "Remember when you didn't have a license for ten years?" underneath a picture of him driving a Porsche that wasn't his. Then people wrote nice things like "Idiot," and "Is this necessary?" below the video of him about to jump naked into a pool. I read articles he posted links to such as: "Study: Sex and Alcohol Make You Happier Than Having Kids and Religion" and "Hucking Vermont Cliffs." I saw many examples of extreme sports, extreme drinking, and just no shame. He was an adorable, fearless, unapologetic daredevil. He was also young, sexy, and completely anonymous. We had no mutual Facebook friends, so he would be a mysterious face that led nowhere, a dead end. Untraceable. Plus he's from Vermont, where I doubt anyone had ever heard of me.

The first night Hunter and I hung out I showed him one of my stand-up comedy routines on YouTube. I wasn't a full-time comedian; I just did it for fun. I enjoyed it but it was like doing drugs: a really high high and a really low low—in other words, an empowering but nerve-wracking experience. I just couldn't imagine having a career where I spent the entire day being anxious about performing at night for only seven to ten minutes. Anyway, we watched my video and after that he showed me a video of him streaking a Miami/FSU football game, for which he was subsequently arrested. I showed him a second stand-up set, and he showed me . . . well, he couldn't find anything else. It was OK. I mean his résumé was short, but I got it: he was nuts. I didn't need any more evidence. He was an exhibitionist maniac, the type of guy who has probably walked on coals or through fire or whatever the fuck. The guy who volunteers to put his head in a lion's mouth—an eternal frat boy who would never turn down a dare. I'm sure he'd slept with half of South Beach, but I liked him. He was cool and even-tempered and easy to be around. And he wasn't a model or an actor like his profile said. He sold coconuts. Coconut drinks, to be specific. He even drove a special van with coconuts painted on it. As if that wasn't ridiculous enough, he also slept in a race car bed with a Zac Efron poster hanging above it. He was a complete alcoholic but very sweet and always smiling. He was confident and hot, and I felt like I could be bad with him and no one except his 10k closest Snapchat friends would ever know.

I was fully aware of how far a situation like this could go, and I was completely fine with that. I had broken up with my last boyfriend a year earlier and was lonely. I wanted something fun and stress-free, something easy. I wanted something that wouldn't make me think too much or needle my emotions. I wanted mindless chitchat, followed by epic orgasms, followed by mindless chitchat.

So time progressed, and this is what happened: I watched him do idiotic thing after idiotic thing. I watched him, via Facebook, get a coconut tattoo on his ass. I watched him pierce his belly button "on a dare," also via Facebook. And one Thursday he posted a throwback picture of his old streaking mug shot. I observed all this in horror and, for a second, I really questioned what the hell I was doing, and where my sanity had gone. I mean I should have been appalled, but I found the whole thing amusing. His antics entertained me. I had a ridiculous crush on him, and I laughed while I took notes. I allowed myself to just have fun, and I opened my mind and tried not to judge him for being an idiot—or myself for being with him.

Did I like listening to club music and gangsta rap during sex? No. Because it's not hard enough to cum without some rapper screaming "motherfucker ass shit" or whatever it is they say in your ear at 2:00 a.m. Did I love the times he was high on Molly and could fuck wildly for hours on end? Too much. We laughed and had great sex, and I was shocked that he wasn't in love with me. But he did say that no one ever turned him on more than I did, and I guess that means a lot coming from the Coconut King of South Beach.

After a month of sleeping together we had unprotected sex for the first time. I felt horrible and paranoid and couldn't get it out of my head. I didn't know if he was sleeping with anyone else, and there was no point in asking now. All his Facebook videos and pictures went flashing through my mind in an instant. I saw the fake blondes with the fake boobs draped over him like wet blankets. I saw him popping champagne bottles on boats while mystery women in thongs laughed drunkenly. I saw my gynecologist in all his earnestness telling me to use a condom. This was not a safety-first kind of guy.

Afterward, he took out a bong and did a hit. Next thing I knew I asked him to blow smoke in my mouth, and he obliged. He did it two more times, and I was high enough to forget that we had unprotected sex, but my eight years of sobriety was out the window. Now I had two stupid things to try to forget about.

This is basically the same thing that happened the first time I relapsed: a guy, sex, him blowing smoke in my mouth. I thought about Hunter and his nonstop partying. What was going to happen to him? Didn't he know he had to grow up sometime? Didn't he think about his health? His liver? The consequences of his reckless lifestyle? How does someone like him keep going on? I asked him if he ever thought about the future and he said no. Quite frankly, at that point, neither was I. We got high together a few more times, and within a month I was buying my own. Within six weeks I had a dealer named Lucky, a glass bong shaped like a penis, and was stoned around the clock.

MY STUPID
STONED LIFE

I went to rehab for the first time in 2007 for marijuana, following a yearlong relapse after having had seven and a half years sober. I signed up for fourteen days because I wasn't willing to commit to thirty. I remember that Paris Hilton was in jail at the time and my thinking that, if she could survive twenty days in prison, I could survive fourteen in rehab. Maybe.

I barely did. I hated rehab. I hated the facility, the counselors, the food, the mosquitoes, and the patients. The only person I bonded with was a twenty-four-year-old bisexual former NYC club kid named Derek, who was engaged to a girl but secretly dating a guy and had done Special K for thirty days in a row prior to checking in. I wound up staying in that treatment center for only eight days, but I remained sober for eight years. They say rehab is for people who want it, not for people who need it. I guess as much as I hated it, I wanted it. And it wasn't a total loss, as I did learn three important things: 1) children don't take after strangers, 2) the fact that I wasn't molested as a child is a miracle, and 3) I never wanted to go back to rehab.

Although pot was my drug of choice, I did have my drinking days, and they weren't ladylike. I had my first drink at fifteen, but drank regularly from eighteen to twenty-six. My drinking story is not that interesting or unique. I drank a lot, slept with too many people, crashed cars, decimated my self-esteem and self-worth, and cried about all of it. I was out of control at night and remorseful the next day but continued doing it because I didn't know any other way to live. I had therapists in college tell me I was an alcoholic and needed to go to A.A., but who goes to A.A. in college? At the time the idea of living without alcohol was preposterous and out of the question; I thought that's what was keeping me alive. As the years passed I grew more and more depressed and hopeless. At twenty-six I met a guy named Sebastian who was handsome and funny and a recovering alcoholic. He quickly saw what a mess I was and convinced me to go to an A.A. meeting. At that point I figured I had nothing to lose. I was right. I had already lost it all and it was time to start getting it back. I stayed sober for seven and a half years.

I'm not one of those people who went to A.A. meetings for twenty years and thinks that they're not an addict anymore or that they can get high safely now or that they never were one to begin with. I know I'm an addict. However, when I took that first hit with Hunter that night, I just didn't care. I wasn't planning on getting high forever like he was. I just wanted to have fun with it for a little while, enjoy a mental sojourn. Plus being stoned was a great time waster. But I still needed something to do during the day.

I thought that, since I was living in Miami, learning Spanish was a good idea. Unfortunately that's easier said than done, so instead I just picked up a few key phrases, like "I'm not friendly" and "My dogs bite." I texted my housekeeper in Spanish via a translation app, and when I got her response, I had to translate that, and the outcome never made sense. Like the time she wrote, "Buenos dias. Estoy Esperanto la puerta eta serrada," which translated to: "Good morning. I'm waiting for the door to be sawed." She also thought my name was Pan, so when she texted me it always said, "Hello, bread!" It was funny the first time, but not the second or third.

Making friends in Miami was a challenge. My neighbor across the hall, Mindy, was cool but she worked. She had a parrot named Coconut who made a lot of noise. What are the odds of having a lover who sold coconuts and a neighbor with a parrot named Coconut, and that both their nicknames were Coco? Although I'm not a bird person, I found Coco very pretty. I listened to him squawk all day, and I thought I lived in a tropical dreamland. Then I went to New York for a weekend and I heard him there too, in my head. Mindy would post Instagram videos of her feeding Coco all kinds of food, from veggie pizza to crackers to mango, and even though we were both home alone all day doing nothing, that parrot ate way better than I did.

Mindy eventually introduced me to her twenty-two-year-old stoner cousin, Lindsey, so then I had someone young, hot, and also unemployed to get high with all day. Lindsey got me into yoga and eating healthier, and smoking more pot. She had a crazy body and long wavy light brown hair that any woman would be jealous of. She was naturally pretty and told me she didn't wear lip gloss because, when she was fifteen, she had a party while her parents were away, and some drunk guy took her lip gloss, put it all over his chest, then smeared it against their terrace door. She'd invite me over to her parents' mansion off Biscayne Blvd on a random weekday and grill us a steak lunch, and I wondered if we were dating. It was funny because there was such a big age difference between us that, had this been 200 years ago, she'd be married, and I'd be dead. That friendship didn't last long though because, within a few months, she moved to New York, and I was on my own again.

After Lindsey left there weren't that many people I saw on a regular basis, but one of the people I did see was my dealer, Lucky. Once a week I'd meet him in the parking lot next to my building. He drove a messy, old pick up truck that I could barely tolerate being in for the one minute it took to complete the transaction. Lucky was an interesting character. He was in his early 60s with a thick head of grey hair and a big red nose. He looked like Charles Bukowski, but unlike Bukowski, Lucky was extremely friendly and happy, to the point that it annoyed me. He loved to chit-chat and would make such a production of explaining all the different kinds of weed and edibles he had to choose from. He got especially excited describing the various flavored vape oils even though I always bought the flavorless ones. I mean who cares about flavors? This isn't ice cream. Lucky was also a "baker" of sorts and repeatedly tried to sell me some kind of weird "cake" that he made. When I asked what was in it he named everything from brownies to cereal to Twinkies—just a mish mosh of shit. It was like the meatloaf of cakes, and each piece weighed like three lbs. I tried a bite of one once and told him it was good even though I found it disgusting.

Despite the fact that I didn't really have friends, I couldn't just sit in the house all day. I decided to try to embrace the Miami lifestyle, so I rented a Jet Ski. Soon after that I heard a story about a girl who fell off the back of one and tore her anus. I thought maybe I needed a boat or a gun, because everyone in Florida seemed to have one or both. The boat idea seemed more fun because then I could pick a really cool, cryptic, or offensive name for it. The gun idea seemed idiotic because I was high 24/7 and couldn't even keep track of my sunglasses.

Things started to get stupid. I went shopping for a rain poncho and came back with a machete. I found a two-inch lizard in my apartment and acted like it was a dinosaur. Every time I polished my toenails, I sat on them. I got locked out of my apartment five times in six months. I found my lip gloss inside a half-empty box of mini Charleston Chews. I followed and then unfollowed a raccoon on Instagram. I got into my car on the passenger side, when I was supposed to be driving. The only thing I didn't allow myself to do was get fat, because fat and stupid doesn't get you laid.

What was happening to me? I used to be smart. I used to be busy, creative, and productive. It's Florida, I thought. But you were sober before in Florida. It's Miami. It's my friends. It's my lack of friends. It's my luck. It's my fate. It's because I don't have a "job." Although I couldn't imagine that having a job would have made me stay sober. Isn't just living hard enough of a job? Then I added up how many hours I'd spent walking my dogs over the past twelve years and realized that I did have a job—I was a fucking dog walker. I hated my job.

Since I had already lost my sobriety, I thought that maybe I should try other drugs. I've never done any drugs besides pot and alcohol, because they scared the shit out of me. I was always afraid I would be the girl who had a "bad reaction" and jumped out the window. Even cocaine scared me, thank god. People were always surprised when I told them that I had never tried coke. I guess I looked or seemed like the type. Because I was thin? Wealthy? Promiscuous? I even heard rumors years ago that I was a coke addict, which made me laugh, especially since I was sober at the time. People assuming I was on coke because I was thin was ironic because one of the main reasons I never did coke was because I was so thin. I knew I would waste away and look awful. I was also too cheap to pay for it, but mostly I didn't want to ruin my life because I was pretty sure I would really like it, and that scared me the most. But now I kept thinking that it would be fun to try Molly. I saw how happy and uninhibited Hunter acted when he was on it—how bad could that be? The problem though was that it looked a little too fun and trying a new drug for the first time at forty-five seemed like an ill-advised plan. Why didn't I just get knocked up by a coconut-selling alcoholic? Or get a bunch of midlife crisis tattoos? Or buy a tiger or elope with another drug addict? Why didn't I just wake up every morning and say to myself, "What's the most idiotic, irresponsible thing I can do today?" I felt like I was on a stupidity binge that was beginning to last too long. I knew I should probably stop smoking, because where was this going? Six months of my life had gone by with nothing to show for it except a machete, a low-grade but chronic cough, and more than eight-hundred-dollars' worth of receipts from various locksmiths.

I remembered the last time I relapsed. The first night I got high it was so much fun, and my ex-boyfriend and I were laughing like crazy. A year later I was crying every night and calling rehabs every day. I woke up every morning and told myself I had to quit. I said that every day for six months, which quickly turned into a year. I procrastinated and tried to pretend things weren't so bad, while I mentally and emotionally deteriorated. I knew there were only two options: I either had to be high all day every day for the rest of my life or get sober. And I knew the former wasn't really an option.

It was now ten years later and I was back in the same place. I knew the right thing to do, but knowing and doing are two different things. I would conveniently "forget" that I needed to stop because it seemed unfeasible. When you can't go to the drugstore, the dry cleaner, or even the mailbox without taking a bong hit, the concept of getting sober seems monumentally daunting, if not downright impossible. Even though you did all those things substance-free in the past, for years, it doesn't matter. You don't know how you ever did them that way in the first place, and can't imagine it ever happening again. So instead of quitting, I pretended I was one of those people who didn't know the answer. I explored numerous time-wasting distractions while high out of my mind. I was attempting to delude myself into believing that somehow I'd find an easier solution to my problems. It wasn't denial; it was postponing the inevitable.

THINGS TO DO
TO AVOID
GETTING SOBER

Dating

Addicts have a lot of problems. We often forget or don't realize that the problem is drugs while we try to convince ourselves that it's everything else. We think it's our relationship, job, money, lack of relationship, lack of job, lack of money. Some of my problems were boredom, loneliness, fear, depression, insecurity, other people, etc. If I could just fix all those things, everything else would fall into place. Well, maybe I couldn't fix all of them at once, but if I could fix at least one of them I would be happy enough that I wouldn't need to get high anymore. Yes, I sort of believed that.

I really hated being single so I decided I would address that first.

I had had plenty of boyfriends throughout my adult life and I was engaged once several years ago. I never cared about being married, to me it was just a stupid tradition that didn't work out 50 percent of the time and ended up causing nightmares and debt. If I loved someone and they loved me I didn't feel the need to sign a legal document promising it would last forever. That seemed moronic. I remember when I was thirty-eight my mother said to me "I worry that you have no reason to get married." She was right. I didn't want kids and I didn't need anyone to support me financially. I just wanted a relationship. Since I was high I wasn't willing to make a huge effort, or do anything that required leaving the house, so I put up profiles on Bumble and Tinder. I decided to keep it short and concise because no one reads them anyway.

Likes: Long orgasms on the beach, or anywhere
Hobbies/Interests/Activities: None
Dislikes: Probably you

To finish it off I lied about my age and included a picture of myself Photoshopped inside a crane machine.

Pam, 35.5

The responses were overwhelming.

Online dating was more of a forum for fucking with people, rather than actually fucking them. I had ridiculous conversations with primitive idiots and started fights prompted by guys' horrendous grammar. One guy wrote to tell me my eyes were beautiful. "Oh, the blue ones?" I said. "They're fake." I don't even know why I was doing this because I was clearly in no position to date. I had no patience or tolerance, and I didn't want to hang out with anyone for more than an hour, unless we were having sex. I sabotaged even the most remote possibility of a connection. My negative attitude and zombie-like persona weren't exactly award-winning assets.

It did occur to me during a brief moment of clarity that anyone I picked in the mental state I was in wouldn't be anyone I would want to date on a not-high day. And on the flip side, anyone who wanted me in this state wouldn't be anyone I would want or respect. What kind of man would spend time with someone who did nothing but smoke pot all day? Either way, I couldn't seem to find a guy with whom I wanted to have sex with *and* have a meal with. I always wound up going back to Hunter. He was easy, convenient, and all I could handle. I kept him around for a long time because who wouldn't? He was the perfect accessory to my ridiculous, going-nowhere-fast stoner life. I asked one of my friends how long he thought this affair could go on for and he said, "Probably for the rest of his life, which at the rate he's going will be very soon." I would wake up early, go out on my terrace naked, do a bong hit, and text Hunter to come over—at 8:00 a.m. And he had a job. What world did I live in? Was I on spring break? I couldn't help it. Pot made me so horny that I walked around like a hormonal teenager in a constant state of arousal. I spent more time sexting than I did eating. My talents were dwindling.

I did manage to go on a few dates. There was the out-of-shape, much younger trainer who made a pass at me and then cried because, unbeknownst to me, he was engaged. There was the guy who told me he was building a log cabin in Vermont (just hearing the name of that state makes me shiver) and that he had a sleeping bag that was good in twenty below. Then there was the stripper from Argentina who I found out was actually a gigolo after he offered me three different types of "massages." He also had three different profiles with three different names and ages. I should have known, but I was high and clueless. He was hot and sexy with amazing lips, and he stared seductively into my eyes like only a professional can. But at $400 an hour, I had to draw the line. I mean I didn't have to, but I chose to.

Then I found Ricky. He looked attractive in his pictures and wasn't awful on the phone, so I agreed to meet him. Ricky was also the name of a goat I met when I was in Morocco, but that's a whole other story, and unlike this Ricky encounter, I wasn't high when I met him.

Ricky was tall and lean and in great shape. He was good-looking, with salt-and-pepper hair, and very tan. We met at a local restaurant near me and, since it was early and still light out, he asked if I wanted to take a walk first. We wound up sitting on a bench talking. Turned out he smoked almost as much weed as I did, so we did a few hits, and, ten minutes later, he tried to kiss me. Out of nowhere. In daylight. On a bench. It was mildly ridiculous and horrendously awkward. I was embarrassed for both of us.

We had dinner and, by the end of the date, he had already mentioned traveling together, engagement, and marriage. Besides that insanity, there were other red flags, but being high, I forgot them. But I know they were there.

The second date we had sex.

By the third date I hated him.

We spent most of the day in bed and, when he fell asleep, I started texting my friend Andrew. Andrew is a psychopath and doesn't take most things seriously. I guess part of the reason I like him is that he's a psychopath. He's also quite handsome, incredibly smart, and gets me. He's seven years younger than me, and he's kind of like the obnoxious stepbrother I never had. We met five years ago when he was single and now he's married and lives in Canada. I still tell him everything.

"So this guy is here. He talks too much but he has a huge cock."

"How do you know?"

"We had sex all day. We argued in bed. He tried to finger me with ice-cold fingers. He wanted to hold the vibrator. When he was on top he had all his body weight on me and I told him he was crushing me and he said he was trying to create intimacy. Everything about him was a disaster. If he just didn't talk or move, if he just let me do the talking and the moving, it would have been so much better. But he persisted. I was happy when he fell asleep so at least he'd stop talking for an hour."

"Did you let him kiss you?"

"No. And we walked past a pet store and I said let's go in and he got all crazy saying how you should never buy a dog from a pet store."

"Tell him to shut up and hump."

"Right. And his phone ring is a door knocking. OK? He told me he wants to get an RV and drive cross-country. I told him I hate RVs. He asked if I had ever been in one and I said no. He asked how I know I wouldn't like it and I told him that I'm a big fan of contempt prior to investigation. I think he's too earthy for me! But the sex is good! What should I do?"

"Do it again."

"I had three orgasms but I had to endure a lot of talking first! He read me something he wrote and I almost fell asleep listening. Do you think this has long-term potential? He wants to write a book with me except he needs to speak his thoughts into his phone. I can't. We're going to get something to eat. I'll text you later."

We went out for dinner and got into a fight at the table. Since I no longer cared if he liked me or not I started texting Andrew again.

"Hey. So now we're at dinner and we're not speaking. He just got mad because I don't eat ribs. He asked me if I saw *This is 40* because he loved it and I said unfortunately yes and that it gave me a migraine."

"He's an idiot. Get rid of him."

"Loves. I think he hates me already, so that's good. He just asked me to throw out my fur coat. He told me that he wants me to be happy and serve others."

"Tell him this isn't a relationship and to fuck more and talk less."

"I know. And he just showed me videos of his dog playing with another dog from 2012. And he whistles!"

"Tell him he reminds you of a dog."

"And apparently he hasn't heard of sun block."

"Oh."

"He told me twice that his dog had diarrhea. And he sings in the shower. I'm laughing out loud. Seriously I'm gonna be single forever. I can't."

"Video it."

"He told me he had a chinchilla in college."

"I'm sorry."

"He told me he's been to 45 states and loves mountains. He stared at me the entire cab ride here. He also loves the movie *Shallow Hal*."

"Why are you still with him? Don't you throw them out after sex?"

"I can't. I wish I had a video of this whole day. He offered to let me live with him and he wants to be my trainer. He told me my body was an 8.5-9 for my age, but he could make it a 9.5 for a 26 year old. Isn't that nice?"

"Lol."

"Should I go on?"

"You should take out duct tape."

"I literally put my hand over his mouth so many times. He told me how he used to take everything personally, but now he knows it's not about him." I stop texting and look up.

"Do you hate me yet?" Ricky asks.

I look down at my phone and type, "He just asked me if I hate him yet. Who says that?"

"A girl."

"He analyzed everything I said. He sounds like someone brainwashed by a lifetime of therapy, or a few too many stints at The Forum. He showed me pictures of him skiing, and the grand Tetons. He wants to go to Yellowstone national park and I want to go to Bali. He made sure I knew how much he hated shopping. He doesn't believe in diamonds. He mentioned four times how cheap his Uber was. He should probably be a therapist or a park ranger. I feel like he's the type of guy that would stare at me in my sleep."

"That's bad."

"Yeah. He knows everything. He said that getting a hobby would make me happy. I told him that the sex we had made me happy and that I didn't require much more. I mean sex takes up as much time as other hobbies that don't culminate in an orgasm. He said he had basically given up on relationships but now he feels differently."

"You should marry him. I mean murder."

"I'm sure someone will. Murder him, I mean. He's just so annoying that it's inevitable. I literally never met a more annoying human being in my entire life."

When I got home that night I called my mom. "Ricky said I renewed his faith in relationships," I said proudly.

"Who's Ricky?" she asked.

"This guy I will never see again."

"Whenever I hear the name Ricky I think of the goat we met in Morocco."

"Yup," I said. "Exactly."

Hobbies

I probably just needed a hobby or two, like Ricky suggested. He's been in therapy for 37 years; he must know something. I mean everyone knows that hobbies save lives and souls, or break legs and bank accounts, depending on which ones you pick.

But what are good hobbies? I could collect goats. I love goats. Of course someone else would have to take care of them because I'm obviously not a goat keeper and don't have the experience, but . . . well, I guess I could read a book or two and figure it out. Or I could get a horse. I wouldn't ride it because I don't get on top of animals that weigh two thousand pounds and could potentially throw me off and trample and paralyze me, but I would definitely pet it. What else can I do? I could learn magic. I always wanted to be sawed in half. Traveling used to be fun, but I couldn't get it together to leave the neighborhood, let alone the country. Traveling is a great way to forget how many problems you have and how much you hate your life at home. That's why it's good to go on as long a trip as possible. The last trip I went on was to Morocco, and I took so much Xanax on the plane that I literally fell off it when we landed. I was with my mother who was like "What's wrong with you?" And I was like "Everything." I had to be taken to a clinic in the middle of the night in Casablanca to get an X-ray. I was sore and swollen, but nothing was broken. A few days later I wound up getting high in the Sahara desert with our tour guide. I don't know what they mix their weed with, but I was so nauseated that I almost threw up on a camel. Traveling was out.

Should I go to law school? Because I never feel like I'm using *that* side of my brain. Forensic psychiatry seems interesting. I googled it and found out that after I go to school for four years, at the maximum I will make only $60K a year and will most likely have to work nine to five in a government building that's freezing, and then I will have to quit. Or else I will have to spend time in prisons interviewing criminals and risking my life for no reason. Oh wait, that's a career, not a hobby. I probably need both. What about race car driving? That's something I always wanted to do. I call a place not too far from me and ask if they have hot instructors, and the guy tells me to call back when I'm serious and hangs up on me. Jerk. I was fucking serious. It's called killing two birds with one stone. Duh.

Then I finally figured it out: chess. Chess seemed interesting and challenging and something useful to learn, because I knew that when I got old I could sit in parks with strange men and play all day. I'm not the golf or mahjong type so I knew I was going to have to find something to do eventually. I googled chess and didn't understand anything, so I hired a teacher to come to my smoky prison to give me a private lesson.

My instructor's name is Sam, and he's tall, dark, handsome, and fit. I think he's Indian, but don't ask. He's very kind and personable and besides the fact that he needed to confirm and reconfirm our lesson nine hundred times beforehand, I like him. He's really cute, and I stare at him the whole time thinking how smart he is, while I grasp absolutely nothing he says. I want him to think I'm smart, but I'm paranoid that he knows I'm mentally challenged and not comprehending. Sam has a lot of patience even though I keep asking the same questions over and over, like, "Wait, what's the horse piece called again?" And "Do these boards come in other colors?" Chess is a great game to learn while high. The question is, If I learn high, do I have to play high? I want to ask Sam, but don't. I actually feel really bad that I'm wasting his time. I mean I had no business participating in anything above the tic-tac-toe level. I was a joke.

Meditation

I told my sister-in-law that I was depressed. I used the word "depressed" instead of "high all day and night" because I didn't feel like being totally honest and having to do something about it, like stopping. My sister-in-law, Harper, and I had a decent relationship, but my brother and I weren't close at all. My brother was a straight-laced conservative businessman and my quirky, uninhibited comedian/designer/addict personality didn't jive with his. He judged me for living outside the box, not working a 9 to 5 job, and I'm sure other things I'm not even aware of. My father was similar to my brother, or the other way around. My parents were divorced and although I had a decent relationship with my father I was much closer with my mother and my brother was closer with him. My mom and I were more artsy and laid back, and hence not taken seriously in their world.

Harper said she had a present for me that would change my life. I thought it was a pink Ferrari with a male model in the front seat, but it was a $960 gift certificate for TM meditation. I had no interest in meditation, but I was afraid that if I didn't do it, she'd find out and tell me I wasn't "trying." I remember a while ago my mother asked me, "What does it mean when people say they meditate?" and I said, "Nothing, just ignore them."

Before my first class I received this e-mail:

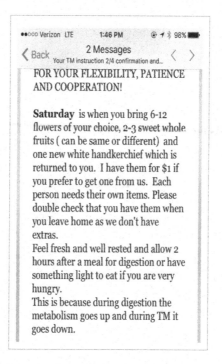

I didn't understand what fruit or handkerchiefs had to do with meditation, but it was obviously critical.

I showed up for the first session so high, because what the fuck is this? The woman who ran the meditation class (see: cult) was an old hippie from the '60s named Kiki, who had shoulder-length gray hair in a side barrette. It was a private session, held in an office-type room in a big building. In the room there was nothing but me, Kiki, and some fake-wood altar where I surrendered my carnation and bananas. This was by far the most asinine thing I'd ever been conned into doing. I couldn't believe these thieves were allowed to do this and take $1000 for it. The place should have been shut down for the sheer ludicrousness of taking advantage of vulnerable and desperate people and promising to change their lives and cure all their ailments. I said that I had to go to the bathroom and walked into the other room to smoke more, even though I had smoked before walking in ten minutes earlier.

I returned from my break, and Kiki gave me a five-minute tutorial on how to meditate. She told me a secret word that I was to say over and over in my head until I fell into a meditative state. The word was so secret that I was forbidden to share it with anyone, ever. If I were to forget it though, Kiki would tell it to me again. As long as she was alive. If she died, I wouldn't know what I was supposed to do.

I can't believe that it only takes five minutes to learn how to meditate, but they drag the course out for four days. I guess if they let you go after five minutes they would have nothing to charge you for and no business. Except the white handkerchief. What a fucking scam.

To be honest, it's hard to tell the difference between being high, meditating, and falling asleep, as they seem like one and the same. I really wanted to tell Kiki: "I don't have stress and don't want to mediate and thank god I'm high because this is beyond stupid." I just can't come back here. Not only is it depressing, it's only thirteen miles from my house but it took me an hour to get here due to traffic, which actually creates stress so therefore it's illogical and counterproductive.

I send Kiki an email before the next class.

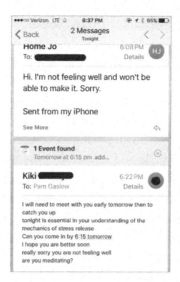

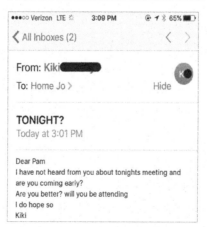

Things to do to avoid getting sober

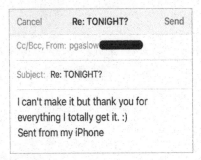

Cancel   **Re: TONIGHT?**   Send

Cc/Bcc, From: pgaslow█████████

Subject: Re: TONIGHT?

I can't make it but thank you for
everything I totally get it. :)
Sent from my iPhone

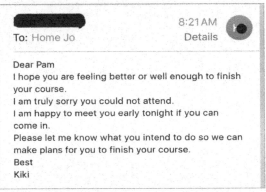

████████████   8:21 AM

To: Home Jo   Details

Dear Pam
I hope you are feeling better or well enough to finish
your course.
I am truly sorry you could not attend.
I am happy to meet you early tonight if you can
come in.
Please let me know what you intend to do so we can
make plans for you to finish your course.
Best
Kiki

From: Kiki █████████

To: Home Jo ⟩   Hide

Checking on you
Today at 12:32 PM

Dear Pam
I have another course starting today in case you want to
come on Monday and Tuesday to finish your course.
Also next week starting the 18th on Monday and
Tuesday the 20 and 21 I have the classes you missed at
10 am
Also I am happy to meet you privately at a time good for
you to finish up your instruction.

I would really love to meet with you again just so I could
feel confident you are going to be meditating correctly.
Kindly consider another meeting with me even privately

warmest regards
Kiki

Her reply to my non-reply:

So for $960 I got a stalker. I was extremely anxious about my sister-in-law calling to ask how the meditation went. I would obviously have to lie. On some level I felt guilty for not completing the class. I had enough guilt living the way I was and now I felt guilty that the thing that was supposed to cure me didn't.

POT – THE SLOW BOAT TO NOWHERE

Months went by and nothing changed and nothing happened, which is pretty much standard in the life of a chronic stoner. I designed a new line of kids' T-shirts, but did nothing with them. I tried writing, but would write one or two sentences then end up staring at the computer in a daze, get depressed because nothing would come to me, and walk away. It took me six months to write a two-page story. I would feel like even more of a loser when alerts like this would pop up on my phone:

I realized that comparing myself to NASA was a losing battle, but still. I had been high around the clock for more than a year. I did zilch all day. I stared at walls. I slept for hours at a time. I did absolutely *nothing*, and may I take the unconceited liberty to say that I do nothing like a fucking pro.

Although I was high all the time, I had switched from a bong to vape pens. I couldn't smoke actual weed anymore because it hurt my throat and was killing my lungs. I also had a chronic, unsexy, worrisome cough. This transition was a plus, as I had already dropped three glass bongs on the floor, and the sound of glass smashing along with the smell of dirty bong water wasn't exactly appealing to the senses. I had tried edibles a few times but didn't like them because they made me dizzy, and I didn't appreciate that it took up to two hours to get high from them. My dog however, had an inclination toward them. He ate edibles by accident, twice, which cost me a ton of worry, guilt, and $1000 at the vet. The first time, he grabbed a piece of chocolate off my desk when I wasn't looking. About fifteen minutes later when he was sort of hanging off the side of the couch in a daze, I realized what he had done. I carried him to the vet around the corner, and they did all the precautionary protocol, and a few hours later he was fine. The second time, he ate half a chocolate bar, and I was terrified because I knew that could be lethal in such a small breed. It happened at 1:00 a.m. on a Saturday morning, and I immediately drove him stoned to the twenty-four-hour animal hospital in North Miami. I stared at him in the rearview mirror the whole time, watching him wobbling around in the back seat, terrified he was going to die. I imagined that, if he did die, it would be my "wake-up call" to get sober. I saw myself sharing the story at an A.A. meeting about how I killed my dog via edibles and hating myself for the rest of my life for being such a careless irresponsible fuck. But luckily he didn't die. And it wasn't my wake-up call. But clearly my life had become unmanageable.

Another reason I stopped using a bong was that I had horrific allergies and thought it was from the weed. I went to an allergist who told me that my lungs were at 65 percent capacity. I was so stoned I looked at him and said, "What are they supposed to be at?" I had turned into the stupidest person alive. I was now the sort of dysfunctional character that I would make fun of. I felt like a complete loser. I hadn't had a coherent thought in more than a year. I couldn't focus on anything. I couldn't read a menu, let alone a book. I watched back-to-back episodes of *My 600-lb Life* and couldn't believe that all those obese, bedridden people were married. I mean I weigh 100 pounds, and I'm single. I obviously needed to gain weight— like 500 pounds. But sadly, in a vein similar to theirs, I rarely left my apartment. I was so lonely, yet I thought anyone who called, texted, or wanted to make a plan with me was annoying. Frankly, I don't know why anyone wanted to talk to me or spend time with me. I was angry, irritable, impatient, intolerant, and rude. If I was in the elevator and someone spoke to me I was literally startled, then annoyed. Like, why are you speaking to me? Do I look like someone who wants to be spoken to? Didn't you notice I'm unapproachable?

Then you know what happened? Another year went by. Another year of the same scenario, day after day. Just me, the pot, the loneliness, and the powerlessness. Nothing was changing, and I feared it never would. I didn't understand why no one was doing an intervention on me. Well, in all fairness, no one really knew the extent of my misery and dysfunction, and it wasn't something I was proud to advertise. My friends knew I was smoking a lot, and while they didn't appreciate the no-warning 15-second pause when I did a hit on the phone with them, no one ever said anything. Nobody cares that you're high. It's just pot. It's not a big deal. Everyone does it.

But not everyone does it to the extent that I did. It affected me in every way: physically, mentally, emotionally, and spiritually. I made a list of the pros and cons of getting high. The pros were that reality and feelings were dulled, food tasted better, and orgasms were more intense. But there were so many more negative consequences. I had dry eyes, stomach issues, and high triglycerides. I was starting to vomit on a regular basis, which was caused by a condition called cyclic vomiting syndrome that some excessive marijuana users get. I basically had marijuana toxicity. I was literally poisoning myself, and it scared the shit out of me. Besides that, I was a permanent idiot and lazy as fuck. I was too lethargic to exercise and too stupid to do anything that remotely required attention or brain use. I had massive mood swings and horrific depressing thoughts. I hated everyone and everything, but mostly I hated myself. I hated myself for becoming this person: for being unproductive, for not using my talents, for squandering my life. All I wanted to do was sleep, eat, and have sex. Ironically though, I couldn't even make out with anyone or give a proper blowjob because my mouth was always so dry. I felt like a useless blob drifting through life. I didn't even care what I looked like. My self-esteem was on empty. I had no purpose.

The worst part though was that I couldn't get high anymore, and at the same time I couldn't stop. I smoked hit after hit until I literally forgot what I was doing. I watched as hours, days, weeks, and months went by. Life was moving forward but I was standing still, merely existing in solitude. I was so hopeless that I decided if things didn't get better, I'd kill myself by fifty.

"First of all you can't kill yourself because you don't have a gun, and you don't know how to work one," Andrew told me when I was sharing my woes.

"Oh," I said.

"So what you should do is go buy a gun, then you need to practice. You should get a target with your picture on it and start with that."

"That's amazing advice," I said, as I sucked a hit off my vape pen. If there had been a counter on that thing I bet it would have been in the tens of thousands. "I'm just miserable," I said. "My life is over. All I really like is sex, sushi, and getting high. And writing, but not always. And my dogs, but not always."

"What's wrong with you?" he asked. "You just turned forty-seven; you look thirty. You're fucking a guy fourteen years younger than you. You have the metabolism of an African cheetah. Blow me."

"What's wrong with me?" I said. "I'll tell you what's wrong with me. I have no fucking life. I can't concentrate. I can't think. I can't breathe. I sweat in my sleep. I walk around with headphones on with no music playing. I wear sunglasses in the shower. I'm fucking brain-dead."

People didn't get it. Pot seems so harmless, but I called it the slow boat to nowhere. I didn't crash a car or end up in jail. I didn't destroy relationships or run out of money or lose my home. But I lost myself, my life, my soul. I was alone all day in my head with my negative thoughts telling me what a loser I am, that it will never get better, that I might as well just give up. I couldn't feel anything. Even if something good happened, I couldn't feel it. I couldn't feel happiness. I had no joy and no hope. The guilt, shame, and awareness that loomed over me 24/7 was like a nuclear cloud. I'd try to obliterate those feelings with more drugs, but you cannot escape them. Being a drug addict is an all-consuming full-time job. It requires all your energy and attention, and it's exhausting on every level. I wanted my life back.

I thought about rehab every day, like how awful, depressing, cold, and prisonlike it would be. Plus sharing a room with someone. And sharing a bathroom. And waking up at 6:30 a.m. for no good reason, and not having sex, and being forced to feel my feelings. I considered doing outpatient, but I knew I'd get high before I went and after I got home. I needed outpatient to be all day long. I guess that's inpatient. I needed someone to move in with me and take the weed away. I needed to be rescued. Then I realized I had to rescue myself.

I tried to stop. I wanted to. I told myself tomorrow I would. Then I woke up the next day and forgot about all that and did it all over again. I'm like a POW, except the prison is my apartment, and the war is inside my head. It was a never-ending nightmare.

I decided to go to an A.A. meeting for the first time in more than a year. I'm high when I go, but I still consider this an effort. I meet two people: a girl named Darcie, who's cute and has ten days sober, and an overweight Canadian psycho named Matt. Well, he's actually Cuban but he spends half the year in Canada, so just go with it.

I noticed Matt at the meeting because he was eating watermelon that he was cutting with a plastic knife and fork inside the container, followed by carefully pouring hazelnut chocolate from a packet on top of each bite. Completely insane food addict. After the meeting he comes up to me and starts talking, and I end up giving him my number because I'm high and lonely and desperate and have impaired judgment.

Matt and I go for lunch. He's not bad-looking—brown hair, green eyes—but he's short and has a big belly. He's a very nice, jolly type of guy; with a beard on he could play Santa at Christmas.

"As soon as I heard you speak, I knew you were hyperintelligent," Matt says to me.

"Ha, thanks. I guess."

He tells me he's a photographer and just moved back from LA. He then proceeds to name-drop several celebrities with whom he used to go to A.A. meetings out there. Name-droppers are always so impressive and not insecure at all.

Two days later I see on Facebook that he's in Canada.

"You didn't mention that you were leaving the country," I texted him.

"Yeah, I told you. Want to join me?" Has asks.

"No thanks," I said. "I have a few things to do, like go to rehab."

"Lol. You don't have to go to rehab. You can just hang out with me and stay sober. It's so much fun. Montreal is amazing." He sends me a picture of a dark street with a tree with no leaves.

"Looks dead," I respond.

He then sends me a picture of Eggs Benedict with ten times too much hollandaise sauce. Looks nauseating.

"The food is good also. Lots of fun. You're funny. Bob Dylan is playing next week. It's a short flight. I promise fun."

Bob Dylan? Short flight? Eggs? Canada? Then he sends me a picture of something that looks like chili but he says is Chinese food. "Time to get you off the block you're stuck on," he writes. "Come explore with me."

I don't respond. Two days later he texts, "What are you up to?"

"Getting high," I wrote.

"Lol, at least you're honest. I actually woke up thinking about you the other night. I think you are a very pretty woman, Pam. You take great care of yourself. If I buy you a ticket to come to Montreal will you jump on the flight?"

"You're sweet but no thank you. I can barely cross the street."

"Haha let alone the border. Funny. There are a lot of intellectuals here. You would like it here. Something about you. You're a goddess. I wish I had met you under different circumstances. Then I wouldn't have held back."

Is that what he's doing? I don't respond to any of this, and then he sends me a picture of a pocketknife with a naked woman etched on it. "My friend just gave me the coolest present ever," he says.

"That's awesome," I wrote. "Who or what will you use it on?"

"Lol. Was just a gift from a friend. He went to an antique store and found a set of eight featuring different women. I wish I had you on the side of my blade. When was the last time you had a real boyfriend, Pam? Do you think you really need to go to rehab? If you surround yourself with someone or people who care you should be OK, Pam."

I don't respond.

"Can I tell you something?" he continues. "I like you because you're pretty and funny and creative and sexy."

"You're sweet, thank you."

"You're welcome. You know the reason I didn't hit on you is because I want to really know you. You're a very radiant woman. I just want to play with your hair and entertain you a bit and be sweet to you. Pam, you are beautiful. You would make such a good companion. I haven't even seen you dressed up but I can only imagine how elegant you are. I think maybe you just need some good loving."

Oh Jesus. Then he sends a picture of himself on a raft in some body of water. "Hate me now?" he asks.

"Umm . . ."

"Sorry. Just wanted to let you know I see so much good in you. I'm happy to be your friend." Then he sends a picture from behind of some woman with long blonde hair, wearing what looks like a white silk nightgown, painting on an easel in front of windows in some high rise with a great view and writes, "By the way, it's warm and sunny here now."

HOW TO FIND
THE PERFECT REHAB
(WHILE HIGH)

Trying to find a rehab when you're high is like trying to find a boyfriend when you're high. Poor judgment usually leads to poor decision-making. However, I figured that, unlike boyfriends, any rehab was better than none.

Florida has tons of rehabs, and in case you didn't know that, all you have to do is drive up and down I-95 from West Palm Beach to Miami, and you will see plenty of billboards that make you aware, or remind you over and over again, that you have a problem that you're ignoring.

- **EXIT 36 – 888 – ADMIT IT**
- **EXIT 55 – IMAGINE BEING SOBER**
- **EXIT 70 – FREEDOM FROM ADDICTION**
  800-NEW-START

The first time I went to rehab I chose to go in Florida. I didn't really know where to go. I just knew that anywhere with cold weather was not an option. I don't like being in the mountains or in the middle of nowhere, so states like Tennessee and Montana were out. I was living in New York at the time, and even though it was June I picked Florida because it was a nonstop flight, they had a pool, and I was high. Turns out those were not the best criteria for choosing a rehab. The oppressive heat, humidity, and swarms of mosquitoes that tortured me daily couldn't possibly justify the nonstop flight and the pool that I never used because of them. Who goes to Florida in the summer? Only a person who shouldn't be making decisions for themselves. This time my only criterion was that I didn't want to go somewhere that would potentially depress me more. This time I needed to do better research.

I decide to call a bunch of rehabs because this is my new job, and another way to waste more time while procrastinating actually going to one. I need to be very thorough, even though I will be high while I talk to all of them. I planned on asking all the right questions. What temperature do you keep the AC at? What time do you wake up? Can you have your phone? What kind of food do you have? Can I have my own room? Can I bring my dog? I am also prepared to answer all their annoying questions about my drug use, and if I've ever tried to kill myself, etc. I have my insurance ID card by my side, ready to recite the numbers, which I can barely see, even with glasses on. Every time I look down at it I squint and struggle and feel like I'm taking an eye chart test. I mean failing one.

After a few phone calls I quickly learn that my insurance company will not pay for anything. According to them I don't have enough of a problem—being stoned all day—to qualify for inpatient treatment. I am told I would have to fail at outpatient treatment *twice* before they will consider paying for inpatient. I'm already failing at life. Isn't that enough? Like, how much harder do I have to work at failing?

I call five rehabs: Promises, Sierra Tucson, The Meadows, Crossroads, and Hazelden in Naples, Florida. Every facility has different restrictions regarding personal items, but most of them are basically the same: don't bring provocative or revealing clothing (no two-piece bathing suits, push-up bras, cropped tops, heels over two inches, or T-shirts with profanity or sexual innuendoes.) Other things not to bring are: illegal drugs, weapons, pets, pornography, etc. Some facilities do not allow cell phones, computers, MP3 players, books, CDs, etc. The reasoning is that "individuals entering treatment need treatment, not entertainment. Since the main focus of treatment should be recovery, outside influences and isolating behaviors need to be minimized." Ugh.

Promises is the original "luxury rehab," also dubbed the "rehab to the stars." It's located in a mansion in Malibu and is the most well-known facility of this ilk. It costs about $45K for 30 days. It features equine therapy, massages, ocean views, and high-thread-count linens. A friend had gone to a rehab that had equine therapy. I asked him what it was about, and he said that you pet horses and role-played with them. You pretended they were your mom or dad or whatever, and took pictures with them, and then, after that, you went in the Jacuzzi and then you got a massage, and... wait, that's a vacation, not rehab. Promises boasts alumni like Ben Affleck, Charlie Sheen, Britney Spears, and Lindsey Lohan. It sounded a little too pretentious for me, but it did sound like a good place to network. I could probably meet my husband there. Or someone else's.

Crossroads is a rehab in Antigua founded by Eric Clapton. When I called there someone with an island accent answered the phone, and I was surprised. Then I was like, why are you surprised? It's a fucking island, not the New York Stock Exchange. Anyway, their program cost $28K for 30 days, and you need a passport and travel insurance. They have a category in their information packet called, "Immigration Department Policy," and it says, "If upon arrival you are feeling physically unwell, you can notify airport personnel that you are a client of Crossroads and they will do their best to advance you to the front of the immigration line." Right, because island people move so quickly, and I'm sure self-obsessed detoxing junkies were their number one priority.

Crossroads offers a lot of the same amenities as other places: massage therapy, fitness, yoga, acupuncture, spiritual development, plus seaside therapy. Seaside therapy sounded intriguing (not really), so I read further and it said, "Every week clients are escorted to a beach for an afternoon of healthy and sober recreation. More than just a social outing, seaside therapy allows clients in early recovery to create positive experiences and memories in sobriety." This is also commonly referred to as a day at the beach.

Under items to leave at home the one that struck me as odd is musical instruments. Is this a place where musician wannabes bring their guitars, hoping that Eric Clapton will be hanging out at the pool and that they can play for him and get discovered? Or do people think that, because it's an island, they can jam on the beach and try to get laid? I really want to know what other instruments people have brought. Has anyone tried to bring a drum set or a tuba? French horn? Also, their schedule seems a tad lenient.

FRIDAY	SATURDAY	SUNDAY
Wake up	Wake up	Wake up
Exercise Available	Exercise Available	Exercise Available
Breakfast	Breakfast	Breakfast
AA/NA Al Anon Meditation Readings Announcements	AA/NA Al Anon Meditation Readings Announcements	Outside AA Meeting
Acupuncture	Flexi Time	
Didactic Medication & Addiction	Didactic Addiction & Personality	RTN Nursing Lecture Stages of Change
Flexi Time	Free Time	
Lunch	Lunch	Lunch
Group	Group	Group/Life Story
Change for Yoga		Family Client Education
Yoga	Beach	Visiting with Family
Physical Fitness		Chores Meeting
Dinner	Dinner	Dinner (Clients Only)
Step Group Life Story/Reflections	Client Led AA/NA Reflections	Debrief Family Reflections
	Movie Entertainment	Movie Entertainment
Self-Directed Time		
Lights Out	Lights Out	Lights Out

CROSSROADS
CENTRE ANTIGUA
USA and Canada 1-888-452-0091 | UK 0-800-783-9631 | All Other Countries 1-268-562-0035

I love how it has no times on it. I'm sure wake up was around 6:30 every morning, although I never understood why they make you get up so early in rehab. Do people who wake up early stay sober longer? Why couldn't the day start at 9:00 a.m., like in the real world? Not that I enjoyed the real world, but it seemed reasonable and respectable.

Sierra Tucson is a well-regarded facility in Tucson, Arizona. They have 14-day programs for $25K and 30 day for $55K. They offer private rooms, but the staff must assess you once you get there before this can be approved. I don't know what they're looking for, but it's probably your wallet because those rooms cost an extra $950 a day. They list a bunch of therapeutic recreational activities, which include equine therapy, expressive arts, a ropes course, and a rock wall. They also have additional services, such as personal training sessions, psychological testing, biofeedback, acupuncture, mindfulness meditation, massages, and a salon. On

Friday evenings they hold the client talent show, which sounded like a great opportunity to dress as a clown or make fun of all the patients in a stand-up routine. Or both. Then, on Saturday mornings they have equine grooming. Why were they trying to get us to work for them? That reminded me of when I was in Thailand and the people at our hotel asked me if I wanted to help them wash the elephants. I mean I don't even bathe my own dogs. Why would I want to wash an elephant? Were they going to pay me? Also, in Africa I saw leopards having sex, but that's a whole other story.

Sierra Tucson has some interesting items on their "What to Leave at Home" list: exercise equipment, craft material, stuffed animals, shoe polish, glass items, metal hairpieces, knitting needles, crochet hooks, insulated coffee cups, chewing gum. Glass items? What the hell does that mean? Like Baccarat bunnies or shot glasses and crack pipes? And no stuffed animals? Maybe they thought people would hide drugs in them? Jesus. Stuffed animals should be allowed, as long as they're not life-size and agree to random drug testing. Other items you were warned not to bring were firearms and narcotics. Does that really need to be stated?

The Meadows is located in "the peace and serenity of the high desert of Arizona, with deep blue skies by day and thousands of stars by night." Sounds like an advertisement for a honeymoon. They have a minimum stay of 45 days, which cost $58K. They don't have private rooms. Sleeveless shirts and tank tops are not allowed. Shoes are mandatory. Shorts must be knee-length. It sounded like a bar: no shirt, no shoes, no recovery, no exceptions.

You might think the more expensive the facility, the better the treatment, but that is not necessarily the case. I found an article in *The Hollywood Reporter* that said, "While high-end rehab has become an inextricable fact of show business life, most people know little about such treatment, which is only loosely regulated, nor how much more effective the luxury approach might be than that offered at such cut-rate in-town options. . . Many high-end treatment centers have a predilection for unproven holistic methods (yoga, equine therapy) and extended stays. . . A lot of them claim to be science-based; they're not."

When you're considering spending $40K to $60K on a rehab, you start to think of all the other things you could do with that kind of money.

Do I really need rehab? Shouldn't I take a trip somewhere instead? I mean somewhere I could bring a musical instrument or a teddy bear, see something cultural, wear tanks tops, make phone calls, and buy cheap and meaningless curios. I could go on five small vacations or one big trip around the world. My mom was going to Iceland and had asked if I wanted to go with her. I normally don't go anywhere cold, but I told her to send me her itinerary and I would take a look. These were the cities (or towns, who knows?) she was going to: Isafjordur, Husavik, Modrudalur, Hveragerdi, and my favorite of all: Kirkjubaejark-laustur. I've never gone anywhere that I couldn't pronounce, and this twelve-day excursion to see glaciers, rocks, and whales just seemed wrong. I was very familiar with the term "Everywhere you go, there you are," and didn't need to take my misery to a freezing country with no strip clubs and 21 hours of daylight.

Maybe I should get a sober companion? A sober companion is a really hot guy who stays with you so you don't get high. At around $10K a month I could get four of them, a different one each week. Of course they would have to cook, clean, walk my dogs, and have sex with me. Maybe I could even get two at a time: as long as they had headshots with their measurements to help me choose. I don't think that's asking too much, and it will keep my spirits up while I go through misery and withdrawal. I mean I've spent more money on less satisfying things. Like last month I spent $1,000 at the vet, and I didn't even have an orgasm.

I had other ideas. I could get a pink Corvette. I asked for one in high school, but my father wouldn't get it for me. He was like, "Who's gonna want it when you're sick of it in three months?" I was like, "I'm sure you can sell it to a cosmetics company or something."

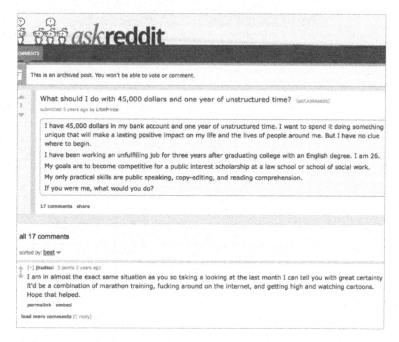

Anyway, while all of those rehabs sounded great in their own ways, I found most of them to be showy and unnecessary.

How to find the perfect rehab (while high)

I didn't need to pay $50K to pet a horse when I can just find one on the side of the road in the local country. I don't like massages, unless the guy giving them to me is really hot and there's some sort of happy ending. Besides, you don't want to go to a place that's too fancy and indulgent, where they spoil you to the point that you don't want to leave. Plus as a general rule I don't think anyone should go to a rehab that's nicer than their home.

I decided to stay in Florida. There was no reason to get on a plane or leave the state. Plus it was only April, so I had time before it got too hot to exist outdoors. I called Hazelden in Naples because it's only a two-hour drive from Miami. The woman on the phone described the place as "community living." Did that mean everyone has herpes? I asked her to send me some information about the program, and I actually read it. I normally wouldn't have had the interest or even remembered to because I'm high and don't like reading and can't focus and don't care.

Done   **Admissions ChecklistNaples.pdf**

benefits. You may be required to cover some portion of the cost, based on you pharmacy benefits. Narcan is a medication that can acutely reverse the effects of taking too large a dose of an opiate and has been shown to save lives. You will be given your Narcan kit upon your discharge from our facility.

o   Family Education group is on Sunday from 10:30am-12:00pm. Family and close friends are encouraged to attend.

o   Patients cook for themselves and order groceries through a local grocer 2-3 times per week.

o   Letters may be received and sent any time. Please bring envelopes and stamps The patient is responsible for notifying family and friends of their specific postal address if they wish to receive mail.

o   Visiting hours for residential patients are Sundays 12:00pm-5:00pm. All visitors must sign in at the front desk. Pets are not allowed on campus including

---

Cook? Next.

That girl, Darcie, who I met at the A.A. meeting, told me about a rehab near West Palm Beach. I look it up online, and the pictures seemed adequate. It wasn't a mansion, but I wasn't moving there. I call and speak to a woman named Barbara who is so affable that I think she is my new best friend. Then I realize that while she is a nice person trying to help people, her job is also to get business from me. I proceed with caution.

I ask Barbara my usual list of questions. Is it coed? Yes. Can I bring my iPad? No. Can I use my phone? No. Can I come for fourteen days? Yes. What is the temperature set at? She's not sure but can find out. Can I have my own room? Yes. I ask if I can bring one of my dogs, even though I don't want to. She says no. I ask if there's a pool, even though I don't sit in the sun or swim. She says yes but you're not allowed to wear a bikini, or you can wear a bikini but you have to wear a shirt over it. I don't approve of these prudish restrictions so I decide not to bring any bathing suit at all. I'll show them.

Barbara tells me that all patients are responsible for their own meals, meaning I have to cook. I tell her to hold it right there and that I don't cook and this is a deal breaker. She says they will get someone to drive me to Whole Foods once a week. I say OK. I ask her to send me a copy of the daily schedule.

barbara.██████████████   April 11, 2017 at 1:33 PM
To: pgaslo███████   Details

▨ Updated contact info found in this email: Barbara ███████████   update...

Hi Pam,

I wanted to say it was an absolute pleasure speaking with you today. You are HILARIOUS ! I have attached the schedule for the mood disorder program. Along with some pictures. Please let me know if you have any questions.

How to find the perfect rehab (while high)

Time	MONDAY	TUESDAY	WEDNESDAY	THURSDAY	FRIDAY	Time	SATURDAY	Time	SUNDAY
7:00-8:00	Morning Beach Walk	Beach Walk / Meditation Management Group	Beach Walk / Meditation Management Group	Beach Walk / Meditation Management Group	Beach Walk / Meditation Management Group	7:00-8:00	Beach Walk / Meditation Management Group	7:00-8:00	Morning Beach Walk / AA Beach Meeting @ 7:00 am
8:00-8:30				First Wave 1/2/Breakfast					
8:30-9:00				Nursing Station Open/Personal Time					
9:00-9:30	Daily Reflection/Goals Group (Peter) 105	Daily Reflection/Goals Group (Christina) 101	Daily Reflection/Goals Group (Peter) 105	Daily Reflection/Goals Group (Christine) 102	Daily Reflection/Goals Group (Christina) 102	9:30–11:30	Gratitude Group Beach or Gratitude Group in 105 (Lindsey/Sandra)	9:30-10:30	Process Group (Sunrise) 106
9:30-9:45	Break	Break		Break	Break			10:30-10:45	Spirituality/Church Depart Lucida @ 8:45 Break
9:45-10:45	CBT Skills Group (Gigi) 102	DBT Skills Group (Gigi) 101	Homework Hour Wellness Center 10:30-12:30	Women's Group (Sandra) 102	Journaling (Signe) THI/109			10:45-11:45	Psychoeducational Group (Lindsey) 105 Spirituality/Church
10:45-12:00 / 11:00-12:30	Art Therapy (Art Affects) 10:45-12:30 105	Break Process Group (Betsy) 102	Trauma Process Group (Joy) 102	Break Process Group (Betsy) 102	Break Process Group (Betsy) 102	11:45-12:45	Lunch	11:45-12:30	Lunch
12:30-1:15			Lunch			12:45-1:45	Psychoeducational Group (Lindsey) 105	2:00-3:00	Team Building Activity or Psychoeducational Group in 105 (Lindsey)
1:15-2:15	Community Meeting (Staff) 105	Psychodrama (Supplemental by Christina) 1:00-4:15 pm	CBT Skills Group (Doreen) 105	Managing Emotions (Christina) 102	Family Dynamics (Gigi) 102	2:00-3:00	Psychoeducational Group (Sandra) 105		
2:15-2:30	Break		Break		Break				
2:30-3:30	Homework Hour / Self Reflection Wellness Center		Holistic Hour: Acupuncture (Dr. Lydon) 105	Holistic Hour: Mind/Body in Recovery (Jessica) 105	Holistic Hour: Meditation (Jessica) 105	3:00-5:00	Homework / Cleaning / Down Time / Gym / Pool	3:00-4:00	Homework / Cleaning / Down Time / Gym 3:00-4:00
3:30-5:00	Journaling 3:30-4:00 (optional) Gym / Pool Time	Gym Pool Time	Pool Time Gym	Gym Pool Time	Gym Pool Time			4:00-6:00	BBQ
5:00-6:00				Dinner					
7:00-9:00	Improving Communication (Lindsey) 102	Outside 12 step, ACOA, CODA Depart Lucida @ 6:15	6:00-7:30 Thinking Chakras (Lindsey) 102	Outside SMART Depart Lucida @ 6:15 (meeting, optional)	Outside AA Beach Meeting Depart @ 6:45 (optional meeting)	7:00 – 9:00	Outside NA Meeting (optional meeting)	6:00-8:00	Evening Beach Walk @ 6:00 Movie Night @ 8:30 Courtyard or Wellness Center

Not surprisingly I don't like one thing on the schedule, starting with waking up. I mean what would I like: a schedule that has sex and getting high on it? I scrutinize it like it's an overseas trip itinerary, crossing things off mentally that I deem "wastes of time." Let's see .. . 7:00 a.m. beach walk? That means I'd have to wake up at 6:30 a.m. to get ready. Is the walk *to* the beach or *on* the beach? Either way it sounds awful. I don't like to talk to people I know in the morning, let alone strangers, let alone walk and talk to them. Art therapy is a gigantic waste of time, not to mention an insult to anyone who is actually an artist. I remember it from the last time I was in rehab. I recall my "project" entailed using Elmer's glue to adhere one-inch foam flip-flops onto a cardboard "God" box. It was more depressing than relaxing.

I try to come up with my ideal rehab schedule. I mean besides a 10:30 a.m. wake up, sushi for lunch, cupcakes for dessert, marathon sex with a hot trainer, and an afternoon at a petting zoo, there's nothing else I can think of.

57

I call Barbara the next day. I tell her the schedule looks boring, but I'm still interested because I know I have to "find God or die." She assures me the program is great and will help me a lot. I agree to do the verbal intake even though I'm still not sure I will even go to this place. I figure I have nothing else to do, and Barbara is kind of fun anyway. She proceeds to ask me a slew of annoying questions.

"Do you have an eating disorder?"

"No."

"Any suicide attempts?"

"Not yet."

"Self harm? Cutting? Burning?"

"No."

"Mood disorder?"

"What does that mean?"

"Depression? Anxiety?"

"These questions are annoying," I said. "Can't you just write 'hot mess'?"

She laughs.

"I mean of course I'm fucking depressed. I'm high all day and I have no life!"

She laughs again.

"When did you stop getting high?" She asked.

"I haven't!" I said. "I'm high right now!"

Barbara tells me that since I only smoke pot I don't have to go to detox, which is such a relief because the last time I was in detox was one of the worst days of my life. Detox is depressing, scary, and lonely. It's the bottom of the barrel of life, where all you have is time to think about yourself and how your whole existence has culminated to this. There were only three other people in detox with me, and I felt like I was in a bus depot in a small town (not that I've ever been in a bus depot in a small

town) with a trio of homeless mental patients. The only thing
to do in detox was watch TV in a freezing room or talk to one
of the other patients, who weren't exactly up to talking. They
were only up to slurring. It wasn't a place to make friends. I had
thrown up sometime before bedtime and felt so sick. I was
freezing and sweating alternately and no one could have cared
less. I explained to the nurse that it was food poisoning and
she didn't believe me because I was a drug addict in a detox.
She had zero sympathy and gave me nothing except a shot in
my ass of I don't know what. I tried to sleep but they came in
and woke me up every three hours to take my blood pressure
and pulse. I had weed and McDonald's in my system, and I was
sure, unfortunately, that I was going to live.

Barbara gives me a whole speech about how I will be living
in a peanut-free house and I am not to bring any peanuts or
anything with peanuts in it—no peanut oil, etc. Who the fuck
brings peanut oil to rehab? What the fuck is peanut oil?

She tells me to bring all my medications, and says that a
guy once brought a bag of weed because that was his "medicine."
Another guy brought a gun. He was from Texas, but still.

Barbara convinces me that this is the right place for me. I can
bring my own pillow, they have a toaster and a hair dryer, and
they will take me to Whole Foods. I can drive to the facility,
people could come visit me, and if I want to escape it wouldn't
be that much of a hassle, seeing that it's only a twenty-minute
drive from my mother's house. It was also reasonably affordable.
Recovery is recovery, and I didn't need any bells and whistles.
Maybe, in fact, I needed the exact opposite. Massages and horses
and ocean views don't really get you sober. I mean the apartment
I live in faces the bay and that hasn't done much for me, so
maybe I need the opposite of that to make me grateful. Maybe
I needed to "suffer" a little to realize how good I really have it.

Then I realize I've been suffering for over a year and maybe it was time for that to end.

I call my friend Mindy, the one who lives across the hall with the parrot. "I'm going to rehab in Lantana," I said, as if she or anyone else has ever heard of it.

"I love Montana!" she says.

"Lantana."

"Where's that?"

The next day, for practice, I go to Whole Foods to see what they have since I've never even shopped there before. I walked through the store taking pictures of what I wanted them to get me. Then I realized I wouldn't have my phone with me so I wouldn't be able to show anyone these pictures. I made a list: fresh flowers, tuxedo cake, raspberry tiramisu cake, red velvet cake, Snickerdoodle cookies, and a large bag of peanuts.

Barbara sends me a final email with the patient contract as well as a list of things to bring and not bring.

What to Bring to ▓▓▓▓▓▓

To ensure that you know what to expect and arrive prepared, we have compiled a list of what to bring and what to leave home that you can use to help you get ready for your stay. We have these guidelines for everyone's safety and to ensure that you will be successful in your treatment and recovery journey.

Personal Items

Documents/Financials: You will need to bring your health insurance card and a driver's license or government issued ID. *You must bring either a pre-paid Visa card, a Walgreen's gift card or cash to purchase toiletries, cigarettes or any additional personal items that you might need during your stay.* We recommend $100 per week for your entire stay. You will need a separate credit card on file to be used for co-payments on medications and any ancillary services that you select.

Smoking: If you smoke cigarettes we ask that you *bring enough for your entire stay.* Vaping, e-cigarettes, cigars, and chewing tobacco are not permitted.

Cell phone and charger: we recommend that you bring your cell phone for travel to us, but it will be placed in safe storage when you arrive. Clients are able to use our phones three times per week, after the initial 72 hour blackout period has ended, to call loved ones that have been approved by your therapist.

Electronics: MP3 players and iPods are permitted if they do not have internet/WiFi access or a camera. Tablets, e-readers, laptops, iPads and game consoles are not permitted and will be kept in storage.

Medications: any currently prescribed medications should be brought in their original containers and will be kept in our medical department and dispensed at appropriate times under medical supervision.

Over-the-counter medication and supplements will be collected and are dispensed at the discretion of our Medical Director.

Toiletries: Clients are encouraged to bring enough shampoo, conditioner, soap, shaving items, deodorant and toothpaste to last your entire stay. Perfume/cologne, aerosol sprays, hair clippers, nail polish and polish remover will be kept in locked storage and may be used upon request. Hair dye, hand sanitizer and straight-edge razor blades are prohibited.

Edibles: All meals and snacks are provided by Lucida. Loved ones are permitted to send care packages; we ask that the food items be store bought, sealed in their original packaging, healthy and healing

Incidentals: Comfort items such as books, sketch pads, pictures, crocheting, and knitting are encouraged.

Clothing Items

Pack at least a week's worth of comfortable clothing, you will be able to wash your clothing in your townhome as often as you wish.

Daily wear: jeans, casual pants or capris, shorts, T-shirts, skirts or dresses (knee length or longer), sweat shirts, sleepwear and bath robes. Exercise clothing and footwear should be brought if you would like to utilize the gym and/or participate in yoga. Comfortable shoes, sneakers, flip flops, sandals, slippers, sunglasses and a hat or visor are also recommended.

What to Leave Home

During your stay you will be expected to adhere to all policies and procedures set forth by the clinical staff. When you arrive at Lucida, our staff will check your belongings ensure the safety and confidentiality of those around you. We ask that you leave the following items at home:

- Weapons, firearms, mace, knives, brass knuckles
- Valuables (expensive jewelry, large amounts of cash)
- Cameras or audio/video recording devices
- Sexual paraphernalia (condoms, pornographic materials, sexual devices, lubricants)
- Sharpie markers, highlighters
- Dice, playing cards, poker chips
- Vehicles and car keys
- Check books
- Laser pens
- Candles or incense
- Anything containing drug or alcohol terms such as hemp lotion, vodka sauce, Baileys creamer, red wine vinegar
- Pets

Brass knuckles? Laser pens? Has this been a problem in the past? I remember when I was in the clothing business and was shipping an order to Nordstrom: it literally said in the shipping manual (which was 47,000 pages long) not to pack your garments with popcorn. I wondered if this had actually been done more than once in order for them to put it in there. Stupidity levels never cease to amaze me. Either way I'm gonna bring some unapproved items, just to document the conversation that ensues.

I called Mindy back. "It literally says you can't bring sexual devices."

"Are you allowed to masturbate?"

"No. They want you to be completely miserable."

"I don't know if I want you to get sober. Will I still like you? Will you still be funny?"

"I don't know, but if you're not happy with the quality of my humor, feel free to defriend me on Facebook. You won't be the first."

I call Barbara again. "No sexual objects?" I said. "Jeez." Barbara thinks I'm the funniest person she's ever met. It's weird how I can be partially suicidal and still make someone laugh. "OK," I say. "You win. I won't bring peanuts, a vibrator, or a bikini. And, by the way, an electric toothbrush can double as a vibrator, if you're desperate enough and cover the head." Then I send her the link to my comedy routine on YouTube.

I felt like I was going to prison. It didn't help that I was binge-watching *Wentworth* on Netflix. *Wentworth* is a series about a women's prison in Australia. I watched at least three episodes every night and then went to sleep and had nightmares about it. I became so obsessed that I thought I was living in their world. Everywhere I went I would think of ways to "escape." When I was in an elevator alone with a man, I thought as soon as the door closed that he was going to rape me. I was on edge, paranoid: fucked up. But when I really thought about it, I knew I was already in prison. The only difference was that mine was nicer and faced the water.

I mean I guess I can do this. I guess it's time. When you think about it, all you have to do in rehab is sit in a chair and listen. Or sit and not listen, I mean at the very minimum.

The next morning I woke up at 6:30 a.m. to go to the bathroom. I realize that this is the time I will wake up next week to take my morning beach walk with my future inmates. It's dark out. I don't wake up when it's dark out. I don't take walks on the beach with strangers. You should be able to get high the first week in rehab to help adjust to your new surroundings and fellow addicts. It's traumatizing to wake up stone cold sober in a foreign place surrounded by complete strangers. They should really ease you into it.

I decided to call my friend Sebastian, the one who helped me get sober originally. He had been sober a long time and had a tough love approach, which I needed.

"I can't go." I told Sebastian.

"Well, what do you want to do?" He asked. "Why don't you just keep getting high then? You know you might as well. You might as well keep getting high. Or you could go to rehab and get help. It's up to you. Which would you rather have: one hour of pleasure or fifty years of happiness?"

I didn't say anything.

"I know how it is," he continues. "We're the same way. I'd rather have the one hour of pleasure. It makes me so mad because I see so much of myself in you. Anyway, I hope you make the right decision, but I'm not sure if you're ready to listen. So if you're ready to change, that's great. If not, we can just talk about the weather."

I am ready to change. I just have one more important question to ask Barbara.

Then the next day:

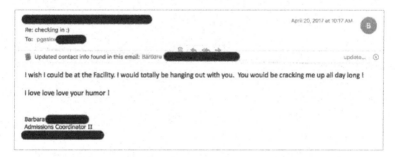

My anxiety about rehab is through the roof. What if my grandmother dies while I'm there? My grandmother is 101 and has been sober for 101 years. How does she do it? She's bedridden, and she's not even depressed! Things aren't totally great, though. For example, when I visited her recently she said to me, "Were you a part of the Egyptian dynasty?" I wanted to say yes, but the last time I went along with one of these dementia-induced scenarios it led down a long road of fabrications that I didn't have the energy to maintain. I always admired my grandmother's attitude about life and wish I had more of the positive outlook that she had. However, recently, she was supposed to have had someone give her a haircut. I noticed her hair was still long and asked her what happened with the haircut, and she said, "I tried and it fell through, and I didn't try again." Sounded like the story or my life.

I called Sebastian again. "What if my grandmother dies when I'm in rehab?" I asked.

"What if you live as long as her?" he said. "That's a long time to be miserable."

He had a valid and highly convincing point. Then I get this email:

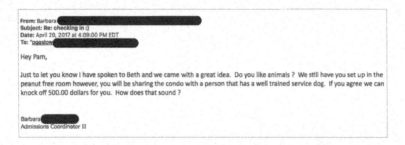

From: Barbara ████████████████
Subject: Re: checking in :)
Date: April 20, 2017 at 4:09:00 PM EDT
To: "pgaslow█████████████

Hey Pam,

Just to let you know I have spoken to Beth and we came with a great idea. Do you like animals ? We still have you set up in the peanut free room however, you will be sharing the condo with a person that has a well trained service dog. If you agree we can knock off 500.00 dollars for you. How does that sound ?

Barbara ██████████
Admissions Coordinator II

Wow. I love dogs and hope it's a Newfoundland because I've always wanted one but never wanted to deal with the drooling and shedding. This way I can just pet it and play with it and never have to tend to any of that. That would be perfect. I go back to my Whole Foods list and add turkey bacon, for the dog. I won't have my phone so I won't be able to take a picture of the dog, but I guess I can just draw it so my friends at home know what it looks like. Actually, I can't draw but maybe someone in rehab can. Addicts are very talented and creative people.

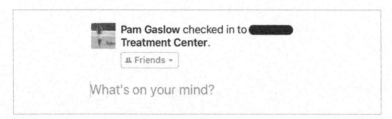

Pam Gaslow checked in to ████████ **Treatment Center**.

👥 Friends ▾

What's on your mind?

REHAB

April 24, 2017

I leave my apartment and drop off my dog Jackson at a boarding facility in Fort Lauderdale. I tell them my name, and someone comes to get him. The person at the front desk says to him, "Take Jackson to North 114." He's going to prison, I thought, just like me.

I drop my other dog at my mom's, and she will drive me to the rehab and keep my car at her house. We don't talk much during the ride. She doesn't get dramatic or worried or make a big deal out things of this nature, which I appreciate. She knows I'm an adult and trusts that I'm taking care of myself. She's going to Iceland while I'm incarcerated. She says to me, "You know what you're gonna miss by not going to Iceland?"

"More depression?" I ask. She tells me Iceland isn't depressing, Greenland is. Whatever.

When we get to the facility we are greeted by an overly tan, annoying woman named Amanda, who is one of the techs. I purposely leave my suitcase outside so I can go back out and smoke more without my mother seeing. This was another good thing about not having to go to detox—being able to smoke up until the last second. I tell my mom I'll be right back. I walk out onto the porch and do four consecutive hits while I stand there looking at my car in the parking lot. I contemplate if I should go back inside or not. *Five minutes of pleasure or fifty years of happiness?* Ugh.

I walk back inside and put the vape pen on the desk and say to Amanda, "I surrender." She looks at the pen like she has no idea what it is or what I'm talking about.

The office is pretty bare. There's a desk, a chair, and a bookcase. The bookcase has four A.A. *Big Books* and nothing else. There is a scale on the floor and a blood pressure machine on the wall.

Amanda and another guy go through my bag (not thoroughly enough, I might add) and take away my hair spray, nail scissors, nail polish remover, and razor. They also take all my medications, including birth control pills and TUMS. I guess you never know when someone might try to OD on hormones or calcium. Then she asks for my phone. I tell her I have to check my email one more time, and I find this:

I hand over my phone and am officially disconnected from the outside world. My mother leaves. Amanda is talking to me but I'm so high and completely numb that I don't hear a word she's saying. I sign 900 release forms without reading them. Then I hear a train go by, but it sounds like it's going through the building instead of past it. "How often does that train go by?" I ask.

"Often enough," she said.

She gives me a canvas bag with the name of the treatment center on it. Inside there's a water bottle, a journal, a pen, and a "stress" dolphin. She says they encourage journaling. Then she hands me a folder with papers in it, which I guess are the rules and the schedule or whatever. I turn the folder over and there's a picture of two people riding horses on the beach at sunset. "Do you guys have horses here?" I ask.

"No," she said.

"Right."

There's also a picture of people pulling up the sail on a sailboat. "What about sailing?" I ask.

"Nope."

RECOVERY. THIS IS WHAT IT LOOKS LIKE.

Turns out they *used* to have horses. They also *used* to have swimming with dolphins, sailing, massages, and a private chef for each town house. Now I guess they just throw you in a room and wish you luck or something.

I pee in a cup, get some kind of alcohol test and a physical and am asked 300 questions about my health. They check my body for scars, bruises, etc. Do I have any piercings? No. Tattoos? I said I don't believe in scarring your body and think that people should draw on paper, not on their skin. The only thing they didn't do was fingerprint me or give me an orange jumpsuit.

Amanda leaves me in the room alone and says I need to wait for a tech to take me to the town house. I look at the clock and it's 14:24 p.m. (rehab time). My life is officially over, and I've never been so depressed. Coming down from the last high is brutal, and anticipating that is even worse. An hour creeps by while I sit there painfully watching the clock. I eat some red licorice that I brought with me. Licorice is the kind of thing you eat until you get sick. I keep feeling a phantom vibration and am constantly looking for my phone, because what else do you do when you're alone in a room in 2017? I feel like I'm in solitary confinement and might lose my mind. Or whatever's left of it.

Eventually someone comes and gets me and takes me to the townhouse. I'm assigned a peer buddy named Jennifer. For some reason I think Jennifer is going to be very young, but she's fifty-eight. She's so nice but the most boring human alive. When I meet her it's in the kitchen, and she is busy deconstructing an Edible Arrangement that someone sent her. She removes all the plastic skewers and puts them in the silverware drawer, as if they will serve some future purpose to her or anyone. I eventually use them to push the avocado out of my sushi roll from Whole Foods.

Jennifer keeps talking and talking and talking, and I want to strangle her. My stomach is literally starting to hurt from listening to her, even though I'm not really listening. There's a note on the board in the kitchen that I pay careful attention to.

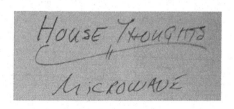

Jennifer takes me to my room, which isn't so bad. At least there's no one else in it. The last time I went to rehab I had a roommate. I don't remember her name but I remember she had a Xanax problem and was married to the only man she'd ever slept with. I found that intensely fascinating, unbelievable, and absurd. It actually gave me anxiety. She also had postpartum depression. I had prepartum—just the thought of having kids depressed me. She was nice and friendly enough, and I wondered if she ever thought about what it would be like to sleep with someone besides her husband, whom she met at fourteen. She had a daughter named Summer whose diaper she changed in front of me on visiting day. I wonder what the odds are that she is still married.

All the townhouses have three floors; my room is on the second. There's a bed, a dresser, a TV, and a small terrace that faces the courtyard, which we're not allowed to go on because they're afraid people might jump. From the second or third floor? Who would bother? I mean the only thing that will guarantee anyone is a trip to the emergency room, and more physical problems to pile on top of their mental ones. If you're serious, buy a gun.

I notice that there's no full-length mirror in the room, but that's OK because I have to focus on the inside, not the outside. I know what my ass looks like anyway, I've been looking at it for forty-seven years and I doubt it will change that much in the next few weeks. Rehab is a place where you learn to live without things: drugs, phones, guns, vibrators, freedom, and now a full-length mirror. I remember the last time I was in treatment, they told us to do things like stare in the mirror and tell ourselves how amazing we are. I guess if I have to do that here I can use the bathroom one and speak quietly.

I put my bag inside but immediately go back downstairs because I don't want to be alone, even though I also don't want to be around anyone. When I walk past the thermostat I'm distraught to see it's in one of those cages—another prison within a prison. If I had half a brain I would have googled how to rig a jailed thermostat before I got here. I alternate between freezing and sweating with random waves of nausea.

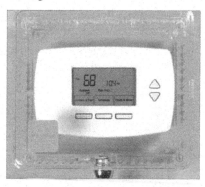

I am sent to the psychiatrist. As soon as he starts asking me questions I start crying. I can't stop crying and I don't think this is a good time to chat, as I'm still high and obviously a wreck. He goes down a list of annoying questions that I feel like I've answered ten times already.

"Have you ever done self-harm?"

"No."

"Cutting?"

"No."

"Burning?"

"No."

"Suicide attempts?"

"No, no, no."

"Do you have an eating disorder?"

"No. I mean if eating sushi every day is a disorder, then yes."

I had been getting asked this question by therapists my entire life, and it never seemed like they believed me. Well, they usually weren't as direct as this guy. Instead they looked me up and down and then casually inquired if I ate right, or if I was healthy, etc. Granted, when these interrogations first began I was in high school and ten pounds thinner, but still, can't a girl just be skinny? I mean I'm open about my drug and alcohol addiction, my depression, and my sex obsession, so why would I lie about having an eating disorder? Yes, God was kind enough to spare me that affliction. I'm allowed to not have every fucking problem on earth. And therapists weren't the only ones who thought this about me. When I was in high school and college a lot of my peers thought I was anorexic, or so I heard. I grew up in a wealthy neighborhood where every skinny girl was labeled anorexic; everyone with money was affected, and everyone who was happy was a liar. The best way to deal with that situation and come out sort of human was to cross the tracks. The "normal" people lived on the other side of the tracks. No one ever heard of a poor girl being anorexic; on the other side of the tracks she was just called skinny. Anyway, I guess you could call me lucky. The only body parts that have grown since I was thirteen are my breasts and my hair; everything else has remained the same size.

Dr. whatever-his-name-is goes down a list of antidepressants, asking me which ones I've taken.

"Have you taken Zoloft?"

"Yes."

"Paxil?"

"Yes."

"Prozac?"

"Yes."

"Luvox?"

"No."

"Cymbalta?"

"No."

"Pristiq? Fetzima? Ixel? Elamol?"

Is he kidding? He names 900 meds.

"Have you taken Abilify?"

One of my closest friends used to be the spokesperson for Abilify and then wound up suing them. So, no. No, no, no. He's dying to put me on something. How about letting me sober up first, asshole?

"Do you need anything to sleep?" he asks. I don't have trouble sleeping but I wanted to see where this would go.

"Like what would you offer me?" I asked. "Xanax? Ambien?"

"Have you ever taken melatonin?" he asks.

"Not interested," I said. What addict gives a fuck about melatonin? I mean why didn't he offer me a warm glass of milk and a lullaby?

Next, he goes through the bag of medications that I brought.

"What's this?" he asks, holding up a tube of cream.

"Pimple medicine."

"You still have pimples at your age?"

I'm writing this all down in my notebook, and he tells me that he gets nervous when I write. I said they encourage journaling. Plus now he knows how every patient feels when a doctor take notes on them or writes a To Do list or whatever the fuck they do. I hate therapy. I've been in and out of it since I was seventeen and I don't feel like it's ever helped me, although I stayed in it because I thought I "needed" to be in it. I have a long history of depression and I've been on Lexapro for fourteen years and it really helps. I also have Seasonal Affective Disorder, to the point where I wouldn't leave my apartment in the winter when I lived in New York. My psychiatrist at the time made me get a light box. When it arrived two of the three bulbs were smashed. Even with all the bulbs intact it didn't do anything except depress me more. I needed sunlight, not a stupid box with light bulbs. After a while I felt like all I was doing was complaining to him and realized I didn't need to pay someone to listen to me complain when I had friends that would do it for free. When the bill came at the end of each month I always thought about what I could have bought with that money, which also depressed me. I hadn't gone to therapy in years.

I keep looking for my phone.

Speaking of phones I'm not allowed to call anyone for seventy-two hours. This is probably a good thing since all I would do is cry and complain and ask to be picked up, kind of like my calls to my parents from sleepaway camp, 9,000 years ago. Glad I've evolved so much.

Later that night I'm in the nurses' station waiting to take meds, and I start burning up. The room is full—there's about ten people in it—and I start sweating through my clothes and shaking. I'm panicking and then I go in the bathroom and throw up. I look down and see red stuff in the toilet. I'm terrified because I think it's blood, but then I remember the last thing I ate was red licorice. Oy. The nurse has obviously seen this before, as she literally could not care less. She tells me to stop dry heaving, as if that's a choice I can make right now. I swear I'm going to die and scream that I need to be taken to a hospital. The nurse yells for everyone to get out. Jennifer gets me a cold wet towel, which is helpful, and I'm actually grateful that she is there with me, even though I barely know her. The problem was that I needed a thousand cold towels. I needed a bathtub of ice. I couldn't stop trembling.

I calm down a little and go back and sit in the main room. I can't stay here, I thought. I need to leave. But where would I go? Back home to get high for the next five to ten years? I know I can't go anywhere. The fear of leaving was greater than the pain of staying. I was fucked. I looked down at the floor and saw the word "SEX," which someone printed out of a label maker or something. Somehow this calms me. Eventually I feel OK enough to go back to my townhouse. One of the techs walks me there and sits with me until I pass out. When I wake up a few hours later I'm fully dressed, and she's not there. If you can do anything in life, don't relapse.

DAY 2

I can't sleep, so I'm up at the crack of dawn. I'm so depressed and defeated. I feel nauseated, weak, and generally unwell. The condo is nice, but I can't be alone with my thoughts. I refuse to unpack because that is too much of a commitment to stay. The impulse to leave is overwhelming. There's a Walgreens directly across the street, and I think I could walk over there, ask someone to use their phone, and call my mom. Why didn't I hide some cash? Guess you can't think of everything when you're high.

I go down to the courtyard. It's so early that I'm the only one up, I guess. The techs have a table there, outside a garage, where they set up shop. You have to sign in every morning and read the schedule on the board, which I soon learn is almost always wrong. Amanda is on duty, and I ask her where the dog is. She says he's not finished with his training yet.

I sit at a table by myself, and a minute later a blonde guy named Kyle comes up and introduces himself to me. He's from Kentucky, and besides his missing tooth he's kind of cute. I mean for rehab. I mean if you like guys who smoke all day, have ten piercings, limbs covered with skull tattoos, and wear cowboy boots with shorts. He has four kids, and his wife is pregnant.

Kyle asks me how old I am, and I tell him. He says, "Wow. I thought you were like thirty." He's twenty-four, and if he didn't have a missing tooth, a wife, four kids, skull tattoos, and a drug problem, I would maybe sleep with him. But probably not.

The last time I was in rehab the men and woman were completely separated except when we went to A.A. meetings at night. They had strict rules about fraternizing. They had the "one minute rule," which meant if you saw a female talking to a male patient they had one minute to walk away. If they didn't walk away, they either had to turn themselves in to the staff, or you had to turn them in. I was like, what is this, *COPS*? I really couldn't have cared less if any of the women wanted to flirt with or even sleep with any of the guys. I figured if they were stupid enough to get involved with someone in rehab, that was their problem.

One of the techs comes over and tells me I need to get blood taken, which is awesome since I haven't eaten and will probably faint, causing another unflattering scene. I learn that the person who takes blood is called a phlebotomist. It's such a big, important-sounding, intimidating title that you should feel like nothing but a loser next to them. They have achieved so much, and what the fuck have you done? Phlebotomist sounds way more prestigious than doctor or lawyer or professor. They should really take that down a few notches. I mean they didn't invent blood; they just take it from you.

I report to the nurses' station and sit and wait for the phlebotomist. There's a strange-looking girl sitting there, also waiting. Her name is Annabel and she has no neck. She insists upon talking to me. I ask her what she's in treatment for, and she tells me she's there for trauma; her father killed himself, and she found him.

I'm shocked and don't know what to say except I'm so sorry. After hearing that, I feel like my problems are now reduced to nothing, and I should probably just cut the crap and go home and enjoy my life. But Annabel seems like she's doing OK, considering. She told me she's made a lot of progress here and that she's learned helpful ways to deal with anxiety. She mentioned some breathing exercises she does, then she added, "And another good thing that's relieving is at night when I walk past the security camera, I give it the finger."

"Nice one," I said.

"So what do you do to relieve stress?" she asks.

"Have sex."

"What do you do for fun?"

"Have sex."

"You sound like a guy."

"I've heard that before."

The phlebotomist is a heavyset black woman, and she has her phone hanging around her neck, and it's playing loud music. I stare at her in disbelief because I can't believe that someone working in a rehab is this unprofessional. Did she think she was at a fucking picnic? Is this what they taught her in phlebotomy school? She starts asking me questions but I can't hear her over the music so I don't answer. Or maybe I did hear her and still didn't answer. My idealization of the super smart, overachieving, studied-their-whole-life-to-get-there phlebotomist is shattered. I didn't even think that my blood was safe with her.

There are two groups of patients here. There's the addiction/dual-diagnosis group and the mood group. The mood group is for people who have depression, anxiety, or trauma. Some people in the mood group are also addicts. Each group has about fifteen people. The drug group is half men, and the mood group is all women. We only mix with the mood people in the morning group and then outside in the courtyard during free time.

The first group of the day begins at 9:00 a.m. They pass around a reading and everyone comments on it, or not, and each person says their goal for the day. Then everyone yells out "Good morning!" When I hear this I want to slit my wrists. It's my turn, and I say, "I don't fucking say good morning. It's never a good morning." "Good morning!" They all shout. Kill me.

No sooner do I say the word *fuck* when someone raises his hand and says that he's offended by people cursing. Really? You did heroin, crack, and cocaine, and drank yourself into oblivion, but the word *fuck* offends you? Fuck off.

All day long you go from one group to the next, with a 45-minute break for lunch, and fifteen-minute breaks between groups for everyone to smoke and complain. I still want to leave. Every other minute I had a legitimate reason. They didn't have food for me yet. They couldn't find a hair dryer. They don't have horses. There's no dog.

I go back to the townhouse during lunch, and Jennifer is cleaning out the refrigerator. Jennifer is the type of person who cleans out a refrigerator even though no one asked her to. She's a workaholic and a goody-goody and enjoys taking on tasks that aren't her responsibility. She's the type of person people take advantage of. Her whole life is her job, and her boss has taken her for granted for years, which led to her excessive drinking, which led to her being here. It's kind of a sad, boring story, and one she unfortunately repeats over and over and over. I feel bad for her because she's already been here for three weeks and she's still doing "work" that no one asked her to do, no one appreciates, and she's not getting paid for.

An attractive young girl walks into the kitchen. Jennifer introduces us, and I find out that she lives in the room across the hall from me. Her name is Mackenzie, she's twenty-two, and this is her seventeenth rehab. She's very pretty: half Jewish, half Italian. She has amazing big green eyes, full lips, olive skin, and long dark hair that's shaved on one side. As good-looking as she is, she's a tad unkempt. Her skin is broken out, her clothes require updating, and she is in desperate need of a pedicure. Jennifer told me she came in off the streets, so it makes sense. Mackenzie's been in jail and state hospitals, and done every drug on earth. I don't even want to imagine what she's seen or been through. I'm sure it's a miracle that she's alive. She's hard and tough, and you immediately know not to get on her bad side. She thinks I'm funny, so I'm safe. She has a very loud, in-your-face personality and a wild dramatic laugh. I like her. I think she's funny and adorable and sad and I wanna take her home and clean her up. In keeping with my prison/rehab analogy, there's a hot but resilient lesbian who is one of the main characters on *Wentworth*, named Franky. Mackenzie isn't a lesbian, but she is bisexual. Mackenzie is Franky. She goes over to the freezer and takes out a chunk of frozen strawberries. She sits down at the table next to me and starts licking them. The sight of this is somewhere between arousing and disgusting, and I can't stop watching her. It looks like she's eating a human heart.

Right before we were leaving to go to our next group I noticed that Mackenzie left her TV on extra loud with her door wide open. I asked Jennifer what that was about, and she told me she left it like that all day and not to turn it off.

"Why not?" I asked.

"Because she needs to learn to do it."

When Jennifer walked away I went into Mackenzie's room and turned off the TV. I knew if I waited for Mackenzie to learn anything I'd be listening to it for the next thirteen days. Call me crazy, but I figured that, with seventeen rehabs under her belt, she was a pretty slow learner.

Someone finally realizes that I haven't eaten anything and brings me to meet Ariana, a short, middle-aged Spanish woman who manages the main kitchen and takes all the grocery orders. I tell her I'm starving, and she gives me Campbell's chicken noodle soup that I burn my mouth on, and a list of food three pages long. I'm supposed to check off what items I want to order and how many. I still feel sick, or I'm detoxing or whatever, and this list is so overwhelming and confusing, like a test I didn't study for. I stare at it for a long time, flipping from one page to the next and back, over and over, as if it's in some language I don't understand. What's wrong with me?

Townhouse:_____ Date:_____		# of Clients_____		Submitted by:_____	
Medical Order for Prune Juice - Medical Order Form					
Please Specify Number of Servings					
Special Request/Recipe Ingredients on Last Page					
Fresh Fruit (as available)		**Hummus**		**Sliced Deli Meat - order by lb**	
Apples - red - each	$0.50	Original - 8 oz	$4.00	(as available)	
Apples - green - each	$0.50	**Hot Cereal**		Ham	$8.00
Bananas - each	$0.55	Oatmeal Regular - 32oz	$5.00	Turkey	$8.00
Oranges - each	$0.60	Oatmeal Instant each	$0.50	Roast Beef	$8.00
Lemons - each	$0.35	**Coffee Breakfast**			
Strawberries	$4.00	Coffee Filters - 100	$1.00	**International Foods**	
Fresh Vegetables (as available)		**Coffee Breakfast**		Refried Beans - 1lb	$2.00
Bell Pepper - red ea	$1.00	Coffee Filters - 100	$4.00	Salsa - each	$0.50
Broccoli - 8 oz pkg	$1.75	Coffee - regular	$4.00	Soy Sauce - bottle	$2.00
Carrots - 1lb pkg	$2.50	Coffee - decaf	$4.00	Taco Sauce - each	$0.25
Celery - 1lb pkg	$2.75	**Tea**		Tortillas - flour lg	$3.50
Cucumbers - each	$1.25	Black	$4.00	Tortillas - wheat 6"	$2.50
Garlic - 8 oz minced	$3.95	Green Tea	$4.00	Taco Shells - each	$0.50
Jalepeno - 8 oz pkg	$1.50	Assorted Tea	$4.00	Taco Seasoning	$3.50
Iceberg Salad - 1 lb pkg	$2.50				
Mixed Greens -1lb pkg	$5.00				
Onions - each	$0.50	**Cereal - Breakfast**		**Misc. Canned Goods**	
Potato - white - each	$1.00	**Refillable Containers**		Beef Broth	$4.50
Potato - sweet- each	$1.00	Cherrios	$4.00	Chicken Broth	$4.50
Spinach - 1 lb	$5.25	Frosted Corn Flakes	$4.00	Tuna	$2.25
Zucchini - each	$1.75	Fruit Rings	$4.00	**Soups/Condensed**	
Tomato Roma - lb	$3.00	Raisin Brain	$4.00	Chicken Noodle	$1.50
Avocado - each	$1.50	**Sweetners**		Cream of Mushroom	$2.50
Green Beans	$3.00	Honey - each	$0.25	Tomato Soup	$2.50
Portabello Mushroom	$2.00	Maple Syrup - each	$0.50	**Soup/Family Style**	
		Sugar - each	$0.10	Broccoli Cheese	$12
Limit One Bottle/pp wk		**Coffee Creamer**		Vegetable Soup	$12
Apple Juice	$4.00	Original Canister dry	$3.75	Corn Chowder	$12
Orange Juice	$5.00	French Vanilla liquid	$3.75	Chili Con Carne	$14
Grape Juice	$4.00	Hazelnut liquid	$3.75	**Fruit in a cup**	
				Mixed Fruit	$0.75
Bars				Fruit Salad Mango	$0.75
Chocolate Chewy	$4.00			Applesauce no sugar	$0.50
Peanut Butter Bar- ea	$0.50			**Breakfast**	
				Pancake Mix	$7.00

Pam Gaslow

Townhouse:_____ # of Clients_____ Submitted by:_____
Date:_____

Medical Order for Prune Juice - Medical Order Form
Please Specify Number of Servings
Special Request/Recipe Ingredients on Last Page

Vinegar		Vegetables		Nuts/Butters	
Balsamic - 8 oz	$4.50	Black Beans - 1 lb	$2.00	Peanuts - 52 oz	$10
White - 8 oz	$2.00	Corn -2lb Frozen	$4.00	Almonds - 3 oz	$1.50
		Green Beans -8 oz	$2.00	Peanut Butter - each	$0.50
Oil					
Extra Virgin Olive Oil 8 oz	$10			**Frozen Potatoes**	
Condiments		**Rice**		Fries - 5 lbs	$6.50
BBQ Sauce - each	$0.25	Brown - 1 lb	$3.00	Hash Browns - 5 lb	$9.00
Yellow Mustard - each	$0.10	Jasmine - 1 lb	$3.00	Sweet Potato Fries 3lb	$6.00
Ketchup	$3.50	**Pasta**		**Frozen Fruit**	
Mayo	$6.00	Pasta, Rings Annie	$5.00	Strawberries - 2lb	$4.00
Tabasco Sauce	$3.50	Mac and Cheese	$2.50	Bananas - 2lb	$4.00
Worcestshire Sauce	$3.00	Elbow Macaroni	$2.00	**Packaged Meats**	
Salad Dressings		Spaghetti	$2.00	Bacon Slices - each	$0.20
Italian - each	$0.50	**Pasta Sauce**		Hot Dog - 1 lb pkg	$6.00
Balsamic vin - each	$0.50	Marnara - 16 oz	$4.50	Italian Sausage - 1lb pkg	$10
Bleu Cheese - each	$0.75	**Chips 7 bags pp**		Turkey Sausage patties	$0.50
French - each	$0.50	**(as available)**		**Meals**	
Caesar each	$0.75	BBQ	$1.00	Meatloaf - Family Style	$20
Ranch - each	$0.50	Sour Cream Onion	$1.00	Lasagna - Family Style	$25
Croutons - each	$0.50	Plain	$1.00	**Bread**	
Bacon Bits - 2 oz	$1.00	Doritos - Ranch	$1.00	Whole Wheat Loaf	$2.50
Pickled Products		Doritos - Nacho	$1.00	Garlic Bread - each	$0.50
Bread & Butter - 8 oz	$1.00	Popcorn - microwave	$1.00	Waffles - each	$2.00
Dill Spears - 8 oz	$1.00	Pretzels	$0.50	Bagels plain - 6	$2.50
Jalapeno - hot - 8oz	$1.50	**Crackers**		Hot Dog Buns - 6	$3.50
		Animal Crackers - ea	$1.00	Hamburger buns - 6	$3.50
		Saltines (WW) -ea	$0.50	**Special Meals**	
Spices/Staples		Wheat Thins - box	$3.50	Salmon - 8 oz	$10
White flour - 1 lb	$2.50	**Drink Mixes**		Beef Tenderloin - $15lb	
Kosher Salt	$3.00	Fruit Punch	$3.50	Pork Loin Chops $6 lb	
Kosher Salt - fine	$3.00	Tea w/Lemon	$4.50	3 Cooked Chicken Breast	$10
Black Pepper	$3.00	Pink Lemonade	$4.50	**Frozen Ground Meat**	
Lemon Pepper 4oz	$3.50			Ground Beef Patty ea	$2.00
Dash	$3.50			Ground Turkey Patty ea	$2.00

house:_____ # of Clients_____ Submitted by:_____

Medical Order for Prune Juice - Medical Order Form
Please Specify Number of Servings
Special Request/Recipe Ingredients on Last Page

Frozen Chicken		Non Food Items		Items Out of Stock:
Breast Raw - each	$2.00	Aluminum Foil - TH		
Breaded Tenders $8 lb		Plastic Wrap - TH		
Fresh Ground Beef		Dishwashing Pods TH		
Beef by the lb $6		Laundry Detergent TH		

Pizza (as available)		Liquid Softner - TH			
4x6 Cheese Pizza each	$2.00	Hand Soap pump			
Pepperoni - 2oz	$1.00	Sponge			
Jelly		Disinfectant Wipes			
Strawberry - each	$0.25	Toilet Paper Roll			
Grape - each	$0.25	Facial Tissue			
Dairy/Liquid		Paper Towels			
Skim Milk	$5.00	Trash Bags		Items still owed:	
Almond Milk	$3.50	Storage Bags qt			
		Storage Bags gal			
Dairy/Yogurt					
Vanilla 32 oz	$5.00				
Strawverry Banana ea	$0.50				
Dairy/Solid					
Smart Balance - each	$0.05				
Butter - 1lb	$4.00				
Dairy					
Sour Cream - each	$0.25				
Dairy				Items not avaiable:	
Eggs - 1 dozen	$2.50				
Dairy/Cheese					
Cheddar - slices 2.5lb	$10				
Cheddar - shred 1 lb	$6.00				
Mozzarella - shred 1 lb	$6.00				
Parmensan - 1lb	$8.00				
Goat Cheese - log	$6.00				
Cream Cheese - each	$0.35	Signature:			
Swiss Cheese Sliced	$6.50				

Do I order an onion? Taco shells? Fruit rings? And what is Raisin Brain? I hand the sheets back to Ariana, blank. I failed the food test. And why are there peanuts and peanut butter on there? I ask her about that, and she says we're not allowed to have peanuts in group but it's fine to have them in the townhouses. I tell her about the stern peanut warnings I received on the level of nuclear war importance, but she doesn't seem to care.

Ariana drives me to Whole Foods. I feel like I have a pass out of prison, but I have a guard following me around the whole time making sure I don't try to escape. When we go to pay she hands them my credit card. The whole experience is weird. On the ride back she tells me that she works two jobs to support her teenage sons, who only eat meat. I feel bad for her, but grateful that I've been on the pill my entire life.

When I get back to the town house I try to "hide" my food in the refrigerator because I don't want anyone to know I have special privileges. I also don't want to explain to my housemates that I'm culinarily inept and that's why I need to get prepared foods.

Later that night I go out in the courtyard. There's a group of six patients sitting at one table smoking, so I sit at the other table by myself. Everyone in rehab smokes; that's the only activity. Suddenly Mackenzie yells from the other table, "Pam, we all think you're really pretty."

It softens me. It feels like no one's paid me a compliment in so long, even though that's not true. I haven't had a cigarette in fifteen years and I find it vile, but if you want to be social you have no choice. I've been so isolated for so long that I need to be communal, even if it means getting lung cancer.

I go over and sit with them and a half hour later we're laughing and actually having fun. These kids are so young, but they're cool and they think I'm close to their age, so I like them even more. I decide to stay, at least another day. But I still refuse to unpack.

DAY 3

I can't believe I have one full day of sobriety. I know it's not much, but it's twenty-four hours more than I've been able to get on my own in the past two years. I'm still constantly thinking of ways to "escape," even though this isn't a lockdown facility and I'm free to walk out the door at any time. The problem is that you can't escape your own mind, which is really what I wanted to get away from. Aren't nine million failed attempts at that what got me here in the first place? I know that pot was just the symptom, and now that I've put that down I'm stuck with the same problems I began with. Learning how to cope with them sober is where the challenge lies. Awareness > acceptance > action.

There's a large cross-section of patients here, which is actually refreshing. There's a former Wall Street executive and a crack whore admitted on scholarship. There's a gay financial analyst from Spokane, and a deli counter worker from Fort Lauderdale. There's also Kyle the tattoo king from Kentucky, a virgin from Brooklyn, and a bitch from Atlanta. Most of the patients are very young—around eighteen to twenty-nine, except for a few women who are in their fifties. None of the guys are cute. I heard from other patients that before I got here there was an eighteen-year-old kid named Josh who was gorgeous and everyone was in love with, but he left against medical advice (AMA) and is now serving twenty years in prison for drug trafficking. Bummer. Actually, several people are here to avoid prison. To be honest, I might have chosen prison if I were them, because at least they cook for you there. To be more honest, they will probably end up there eventually anyway.

Last time I was in rehab there was a middle-aged, weathered crackhead named Annie who had been to treatment seven times and was there to avoid jail. When she checked in she had pills taped up and down her arms underneath her sweatshirt. People just don't listen. There is a list of things you are *not* supposed to bring to rehab, like guns, knives, your cats, and *drugs*. Every time she took something out of her suitcase more pills fell on the floor. I knew within the first week she would either be thrown out, OD, or get sent to the psych ward. Five days later her "boyfriend" met her outside and tossed a bottle of pills over the wall. She got kicked out and everyone was happy because they thought she was distracting. I personally found her amusing. Right before she left she said to me, "Oh Pam, you would love crack. When you get out of here call me. We'll go out and have Bahama mamas."

Everyone in rehab is nuts in one way or another, but the ones with potential jail time looming over them intrigued me because they obviously took it to the next level. No one knew what they had done. It was just known that they were one false move away from incarceration. One of the people in this exclusive club was Melanie, the bitch from Atlanta. When I call her a "bitch" I mean she just seemed perpetually miserable and angry, like someone who hasn't had sex in years and might explode at any moment. Melanie acted like the mother of the group—sticking up for everyone's rights and trying to be the mediator in all disagreements. She's not the oldest, but she's been here the longest: four months, which really means nothing except that she's probably smoked the most cigarettes.

The other person avoiding jail time was Justin. Justin was the deli counter worker, and he's only eighteen. He sports a Batman earring in each ear and wears flip-flops with socks every day. He seems harmless but who knows what these people are capable of when they're high? He's not too bright, and he bores me by bragging about all the girls he's slept with. It's entirely insecure, unimpressive, and annoying. He sits next to me in every group and flirts with me, which I repeatedly pretend not to notice. He's nice but he smells like an ashtray.

Every day in group you have to say how you feel, and you can't say "good" or "fine" or "OK," because those are not feelings. "Fine" actually means fucked up, insecure, neurotic, and emotional. Ugh. "Fear" means fuck everything and run or face everything and recover. "Relationship" means really exciting love affair turns into outrageous nightmare, sobriety hangs in peril, so good luck with that. It's annoying to come up with a feeling every day but you just make one up so they will pass to the next person, who also makes one up. Ezra is the virgin from Brooklyn, and he never knows how he feels. He's also eighteen but he looks like an old man: short and pudgy and prematurely balding. He's a sweet guy and always smiling, but he's not the brightest either. For example, this is his fourth rehab in thirty days. He got kicked out of the first three for fighting. His teeth are yellow and black, which is a remarkable achievement for a teenager.

"What's your drug of choice?" Ezra asks me after group that day.

"Pot," I said.

"That's it?" He asks.

"Is that not a drug?"

This keeps happening. When I tell people I'm here for pot they basically laugh at me. That's nice. Idiots. I love how one drug isn't enough, especially if it's pot. Potheads are not even considered addicts by other hardcore addicts. I used to resent the fact that *Intervention* would never do a show about someone like me. Pot isn't exciting enough. It's not gritty or dirty or fascinating, or even interesting. No one thinks it's a drug, let alone one that can screw up your entire existence. Well, I haven't had a drink in more than twenty years, and I'm a fucking mess. Yes, I wasn't going to die from pot, but believe me I couldn't feel any more dead inside. For most people taking a hit of weed meant some laughs and a temporary escape from reality, for me it meant giving up on life.

That afternoon I have the first meeting with my therapist. Her name is Stephanie, and she appears to be around the same age as me. She has pretty green eyes, a round face, and long, thick brown hair that I'm envious of. I wonder if she's single, and if not, if she's lonely. I wonder if by being a therapist she has solved all her own problems. Maybe I should be a therapist. I mean once I solve my problems like I assume Stephanie has. I wonder how long that takes.

I feel ten times better sitting in front of Stephanie than I did the first day when I met with the psychiatrist. I'm more clearheaded and able to listen. It's kind of pertinent to not be high when you're trying to deal with why you were getting high. The questions begin again.

"Have you ever harmed yourself?" Stephanie asks.

"No," I said.

"Cutting?"

"No."

"Burning?"

"No."

Can't they put this information in a database so we don't have to be asked the same questions over and over again by every therapist here?

"Ever been suicidal?" She asks.

"I mean I read *Final Exit*."

"Have you ever prostituted yourself?"

"For *pot*?"

She laughs, then asks me to tell her why I'm here. I hate the pressure of feeling like there's a clock over my head, and that I need to vomit my life story on someone who's never met me as quickly as possible, so that she at least has time to respond before the session is over. How do you sum up forty-seven years in forty-five minutes? I guess you do the best you can.

"In a nutshell I've been smoking pot around the clock for two years. I'm lonely and depressed and totally isolated. I don't work and have nothing to do all day. I was in the clothing business for almost ten years and I think about getting back into it, but what if it doesn't work out? I also want to write a book, but what if it doesn't get published? I've lost my self-esteem and myself and can't get out of my own way. I tried to fill all these voids with pot and it didn't work and now I'm here. Help."

She takes a minute to process this. Then she says, "Has anyone ever told you that you're a perfectionist?"

"No."

A perfectionist? What does that have to do with anything? Do they just throw labels out at you? She doesn't even know me. Then I think about it. When I get honest with myself I have to admit that I've been lost since I closed my clothing business. I kind of defined myself by my success in that. I've wanted to start something new, but I've been afraid it won't work. However if I don't do it, it won't work, so I don't do it and it doesn't work. It's a self-defeating self-fulfilling prophecy. I'm afraid of failure so I don't try, then I'm upset because I'm not succeeding. Then I hide behind drugs. Or try to. I guess it's time to stop living in fear. I guess it's time to face everything and recover.

I was surprised that with all my years of therapy that no one ever said this to me before. I thought more about the perfectionism . . . I mean I don't make my bed in the morning because I can't do it like they do in hotels, so why bother? I've had every freckle (brown spot/sun damage) lasered off my face five times. I can't finish decorating my apartment because I can't find the perfect accessories. I tell people not to look at the right side of the living room because it's not finished yet, and I don't want them to judge me on something that's not complete. I haven't done any walking since I got here because I can't count my steps because I don't have my phone, and what's the point of walking if you don't know how far you've gone? Maybe Stephanie is onto something. I mean she is a therapist. Ugh.

"Have you heard of foreboding joy?" Stephanie asks me.

"No," I said, "but it sounds like a term I should have invented."

She tells me about a book I should read, called *Daring Greatly*, and lends me her copy. For homework I have to write down all the reasons I got high. I wish I could do this assignment in Photoshop or iMovie, or even as a stand-up routine, but unfortunately those options aren't available to me here in drug prison.

I had so many reasons to get high. I was bored, lonely, and depressed. I wasn't having enough "fun." People sucked. Life was disappointing. The weather was bad, or good. All holidays were valid: Christmas, with its super-annoying jingles and expected cheer, New Year's because it's another fucking year of the same shit, and Halloween, with adults acting like a bunch of idiots dressed up as hot dogs or toilet paper, or whatever the fuck. It was Monday, Tuesday, Wednesday, Thursday, Friday. It was my birthday. My grandmother died (four years ago, but still). I'm single. I live in Miami. My dogs are annoying, untrained con artists. I had unprotected sex and needed to obliterate that from my mind. My bathroom faucet leaks. My dryer is broken. I'm gonna be fifty (in three years, but still.) I'm afraid of the future. My dogs are getting old. My parents are getting old. I'm getting old. I hate everything.

That night I start looking through the book Stephanie gave me and found some interesting thoughts.

> Perfectionism is not about healthy achievement and growth. Perfectionism is a defensive move. It's the belief that if we do things perfectly and look perfect, we can minimize or avoid the pain of blame, judgment, and shame. Perfectionism is a twenty-ton shield that we lug around, thinking it will protect us, when in fact it's the thing that's really preventing us from being seen.

Perfectionism is not the key to success. In fact, research shows that perfectionism hampers achievement. Perfectionism is correlated with depression, anxiety, addiction, and life paralysis or missed opportunities. The fear of failing, making mistakes, not meeting people's expectations, and being criticized keeps us outside of the arena where healthy competition and striving unfolds.

Then I read this quote by Gretchen Rubin who wrote in *The Happiness Project*:

I remind myself, "Don't let the perfect be the enemy of the good (Voltaire). A twenty-minute walk that I do is better than the four-mile run that I don't do. The imperfect book that gets published is better than the perfect book that never leaves my computer. The dinner party of take-out Chinese food is better than the elegant dinner that I never host."

Three ways to shield from vulnerability: foreboding joy, or the paradoxical dread that clamps down on momentary joyfulness; perfectionism, or believing that doing everything perfectly means you'll never feel shame; and numbing, the embrace of whatever deadens the pain. The problem is "we can't selectively numb emotion. Numb the dark and you numb the light."

I guess Stephanie didn't just throw a term out at me. I think Stephanie knows me better than I know myself.

DAY 4

There's a saying that if everyone puts his or her problems in the middle of the table, you'll always take yours back. No place is that a more accurate statement than in a drug rehab. During the morning meeting some girl in the mood group says that her goal for the day is not to get bitten by a squirrel, like she did the day before. I'm sorry, but did my brain just break? Is there a video of this supposed biting? Were there any eyewitnesses? If this is even a true story she was obviously feeding the squirrel, since they don't just walk up to you and bite. I hope she fed it a peanut. Fucking idiot.

Everyone in treatment is on some kind of medication, and if you're not, they put you on one or two, or thirty. Each patient needs to be medicated or the staff isn't happy. Some people are overmedicated, and some are trying to get overmedicated. Meds are dispensed three times a day at the nurses' station. I only take medication in the morning (Lexapro, which I had been on for fourteen years, and birth control which I'd been on forever), and if you get there late you could wait forever. The first time I went I waited thirty-five minutes to swallow three pills. After that I started waking up early so I could be the first one there. I didn't have to set an alarm because Mackenzie's alarm clock woke up everyone in the entire house, except Mackenzie. I also learned from being up at the crack of dawn that no one goes on the morning beach walks, except Jennifer. Glad I spent so much time worrying about them.

The nurses have a list of everyone's medications, and you have to initial next to the name of each one after you take it. Rather than hand you a single pill, they hand you the whole bottle, so you could technically swallow all of them, but whatever.

Rehab

They also take your blood pressure every time. My blood pressure is really low, and my doctor at home once asked me if I was alive after taking it. I said no.

While in the nurses area I meet a new girl named Meadow. She's very fair skinned with freckles and has no makeup on. She's tall and thin and her thick black curly hair is piled on top of her head. She's eighteen years old and looks completely terrified and sad. She tells me she hates it here and wants to go home. I tell her I know exactly how she feels, and not to brag but I threw up in front of everyone only a few nights ago, so compared to that she's doing great. She said that she refused to even leave her room for her first few hours here, and said no one even came to look for her. Now she was out of hiding and waiting to get her blood taken.

"I told my mom this is like a retirement home," Meadow said. She has her journal open on her lap. When she's not looking I peek over, and it says, "My first day in hell."

After talking for a little while she opens up and says not to tell anyone, but her father is one of the main characters from *Breaking Bad*. Her parents are divorced and she was raised by nannies in Bel Air. She said a fan wrote her dad a letter on Facebook and he reached out to her and now they're married. If I knew shit like that really worked I would have stalked way harder in my twenties and thirties. Ugh.

The same phlebotomist who took my blood is taking Meadow's, but this time her music is off. I watched as she went to work on her. She filled a vial with her blood, and then she dropped it on the floor, and we both watched it roll away. Meadow turned around to look at me and I shook my head. No bueno.

Some days the groups are more helpful than others. Some days you learn new things, some days you're reminded of old things you forgot, and some days you're just bored and watching the clock and wondering what the fuck this has to do with getting sober. Today was one of those days. The first thing the counselor had us do was make a list of things we hate. That's easy:

1) Squirrels
2) Saying "good morning"
3) Making lists
4) Rehab

Then he suggests that we make a dream book. Does he mean the dreams we have at night or the dreams we wish for? Sometimes I have orgasms in my sleep, but I'm sure no one wants to hear about that. Do they?

He also suggests having a God box. A God box is a place where you put your problems or worries or whatever you want God to handle for you. I wish I could put my dogs in my God box, but they're so annoying I doubt God wants them either. You probably think that's a crazy idea, but the truth is that you can put anything in your God box, as long as it fits. I plan on making mine the size of a small kennel, so it shouldn't be a problem. The only things you can't put in there are your bills; God doesn't like that.

Finally, the counselor tells us to name five things that are good in our lives. It's Mackenzie's turn and she says, "My dog. My other dog—do they count as one? Does my cat count?"

Ezra interrupts her, "Can I just say one thing?" he asks. Ezra has this incessant need to be the center of attention. He constantly interrupts everyone, including the therapist. "Can I just say one thing?" is his standard interjection, which is always followed by: "To be totally honest. . . ." This happens all the time but the counselors eventually tell him to just shut up and listen, like he's in first grade. I mean Mackenzie is loud and attention-seeking but in a more amusing, less rude way than Ezra. Last time I was in rehab some people were forced to wear signs. I remember the annoying crackhead had to wear one that said: "I'm practicing silence." That would be a great sign for Ezra. If there were a suggestion box I'd put that in it. Maybe I could put it in my God box that they get a suggestion box. Everyone would thank me and God, but mostly me because it was my idea.

Anyway, Ezra says his one thing, Mackenzie finishes her list, and then it's Justin's turn. He shares that he loves his dirt bike, his video games, and a few other things I don't remember. He says that he's naturally high, but when he's depressed he plays Christmas music in his head. If he's naturally high, then why did he do drugs and what is he doing here? He needs to think about that. And who the fuck likes Christmas music? I literally run out of stores when they play it because I find it so depressing. Mackenzie looks at me when he says that, and I know she's thinking the same thing. Every time someone says something ridiculous she stares at me with wide eyes and I feel like I have a buddy. I mean a real buddy, not an assigned one who cleans out refrigerators.

I'm finally allowed to make phone calls. Phone calls are permitted three times a week for twenty minutes, and you can only call people on your approved calling list. A tech dials for you and stands over you while you talk. There's a six-digit code to dial out, and they have the screen covered with black tape so you can't see the number. Last time I was in rehab there was one payphone that fifteen girls shared: fifteen selfish, self-absorbed drug addicts, who all thought their time was more important than anyone else's. There was a timer outside the phone room that you were supposed to set for fifteen minutes, except when fifteen minutes was up people reset it for another five and another five, etc. I would hear girls fighting like animals on the phone, screaming and crying. I remember one night the crackhead wanted to use the phone, and she started telling the person on it to hurry up. The girl didn't listen, and then she gave her the "Do you know who I am?" line. The girl on the phone hung up with whomever she was speaking to and said, "Yeah. You're an addict in a rehab," and coolly walked away. Then she went in the payphone booth and set the timer for thirty minutes—fifteen to scream at her mom, and fifteen to scream at her boyfriend.

Anyway, having the phones monitored by the techs seems more civilized and less likely to end in an argument, at least not between patients. The tech hands me a phone list and asks me who I want to call first. The only problem is it's not my list. I look over the names and say, "Let's call Scott Mulholand; he sounds nice."

The problem with calling people from rehab is that the number is blocked, or shows up as some weird number that no one will answer, so you have to leave a voice mail telling whoever that it's you and to answer the next time they see a number they don't recognize. This game is really fun, and you often end up speaking to no one. Fortunately though, my dad did answer. I talked to him for a few minutes and then hear Meadow crying hysterically on the phone next to me. I tell him to hold so I can eavesdrop more effectively.

"It's like prison here," Meadow cries. "It's a horrible place, like a Woodstock rec room. They treat you like dogs and everyone smokes. Mom, this place is like a reality show."

It's better than a reality show I thought, because it's actually real. Poor Meadow. She keeps saying that she will probably leave and go to a rehab in Malibu. She needs horses and massages and ocean views to get better. This place is a dump, and that just won't work for her.

Before bed everyone sits outside and smokes and talks. Since we don't have phones or computers or sexual devices, we are forced to socialize with each other. I hang out for an hour or so, and then one of the techs comes over and tells me I have to unpack because they need to put my suitcase in storage. I tell him I have no problem storing it in my closet, and he says no. I go upstairs and unpack. I bring the empty suitcase back downstairs, then I go back to my room and watch the ID channel. I switch to HSN2 and they're selling a Debbie Meyer green rectangular cake box. It says press OK to shop. Who the fuck is Debbie Meyer? I press OK and nothing happens. I normally don't even watch TV, but the lighting is so bad here that I can't read a book or floss my teeth with any real accuracy.

Day 5

Every morning I see Jennifer on the way to get my meds, and she tells me the same story about setting boundaries with her boss. It's so repetitive and monotonous but I have to listen because I have nowhere else to go, and she saved my life the first night with the wet towels.

Everyone has a journal, and people are always scribbling in them all day long. What are they writing? I mean I'm writing about them, but what are they writing about? I get to the morning group early, and the girl next to me is writing feverishly in her journal. I peek over and it says, "Benefit mascara" under "Characteristics of a healthy relationship." Mystery solved.

Before group starts we find out that Meadow left. No one knows where she went but I'm assuming back to California to be with her mother. Her next stop will be a rehab for the entitled children of movie stars. White glove or bust.

The group starts, and the girl who said her goal the day before was not to get bitten by a squirrel says that her goal for the day is to be an avocado. I feel like I'm at a fucking carnival. I realize that not every moment here is going to be an epiphany and that I have to just "trust the process," but is anyone paying attention to this? Can someone save her?

Once a week we have a community group meeting, which they define as "airing your grievances," but it's really just an opportunity for everyone to complain about each other or the staff. It starts off with the guys whining about how Ezra doesn't help with the cooking or cleaning in the house and expects everything to be done for him. Ezra's says he wasn't told prior to checking in that he would have to cook his own food and he doesn't know how. A few other people chime in and say the same thing, and I concur as well, even though I did know. I just think it's stupid. People come to treatment with enough stress and anxiety, and having to cook your own meals is just more shit to deal with. Anyway, that's not my issue. My issue is that they should remove the horses from the back of their admissions folders. Or get horses.

Among other trivial issues, people complain that they're not getting their mail in a timely manner. Umm, it's 2017. Make a fucking phone call! I can't believe people actually still write letters. Did they also take a horse and buggy to get here? Another interesting grievance is that we don't have enough free time. Didn't everyone have enough free time getting drunk and high before they got here? What exactly do they need free time for? We can't use any electronic devices or masturbate or get a manicure, so what do they want to do? I mean do they see any horses or sailboats or Ferris wheels around here? Does this look like Malibu? Sorry kids, you used up all your free time in the worst ways possible. This isn't a vacation. It's rehab.

Rehab

After group, Catherine, a woman in her late fifties, comes up to me and tells me she has some great recipes for me. Umm, I don't think my lack of recipes is the reason I don't cook. She gives me a recipe for sweet potatoes, which requires slicing them. I'm barely strong enough to cut an apple in half. She tells me to just press the "sweet potato" button on my microwave but my microwave doesn't have a sweet potato button, so I'm lost. Even if I wanted to cut a potato, or anything for that matter, there are no sharp knives in the kitchen. Like I mentioned they take any potentially dangerous objects away from you when you check in. If you want to use your razor or deadly hair spray someone has to come up and unlock the pantry, sign it out, then sign it back in. You can sign a knife out for twenty minutes. That's definitely long enough to stab everyone here and return it, perfectly spotless.

On my way back to the town house for lunch I recognize a therapist from the treatment center I went to ten years ago. "Hey," I said, "I remember you from the Hanley Center."

She seems startled as if she just got found out or something. I remember when I'd met her she was so insanely positive and enthusiastic. "I love my job," she'd said, "I looooove what I do."

"Great," I'd said, wanting to vomit. We'd spoken for a while. "You are very smart," she'd said, "brilliant."

"Yes," I'd said, "it's all great but it's landed me here."

Then she reached into her desk drawer and took out—wait for it—a plastic magic wand and waved it over my head. All I could think was: is this for real? Am I really paying $1,000 a day for this? Is this what they teach you in drug counselor school? It was literally too insane to even tell anyone. It's like saying the Magic 8 Ball is my therapist.

"You waved a magic wand over my head," I said. "It obviously didn't work."

"You have to look within," she said. Figures. Therapists have an answer for everything. She may be right, but she should still be arrested. Or committed. Fucking kook.

That afternoon we have group with a counselor named Mike. He's also a recovering addict, and he's very direct. It's the first time I'm meeting him so he asks who I am and why I'm here. I repeat my super-fascinating story.

"I've literally done nothing but get high for the past two years," I said, starting to cry. "I feel like such a loser."

"Really?" he said. "Have you lost the ability to help someone else?"

Wow.

Silence.

"I guess not," I said. And at that moment I had a modicum of hope. I guess I needed to be reminded that I'm not totally useless. I really never thought about anyone else when I was high. How could I? "Selfishness, self-centeredness—that we believe is the root of all our problems."

"Listen," he said, "you're here. Just by getting here you've done 50 percent of the job. So stop beating yourself up."

I realized that beating myself up had practically become my full-time job. I excelled at it. I hated myself so I got high, then I hated myself more for getting high. I was finally off that destructive merry-go-round and needed to quit that job. I needed to start liking myself again. I remember when I first got sober at twenty-six, they told me that you get self-esteem by doing estimable things. Instead of feeling like a loser for being here, I should feel like a winner for getting here. Instead of hating myself for being high for so long, I should like myself for finding the courage to quit. It's all about perspective, and mine always sucked.

"Did you get high today?" Mike asks.

"No," I said.

"Then you're a winner. That's all you have to do."

"I guess."

"You're your own worst enemy," he said. "Would you let someone talk to you the way you talk to yourself?"

"No."

"It's time to start being nice to yourself," he said. "It's time to retrain your brain."

After group we have a cooking lesson with the resident dietician. He asks if anyone has cooked anything interesting this week. Is this culinary school? Who the fuck cares? Coffee and cigarettes are the primary food groups for recovering addicts, so I'm not sure he's gonna get an encouraging answer. He shows us how to make a smoothie. He puts spinach, nuts, a banana, coconut water, and protein powder into a blender, and the end result looks like mud. Is this cooking? Someone raises their hand and asks if you can replace the protein powder with fish, and I almost throw up. You can put all the healthy shit in the world in your smoothies but you all smoke 9,000 cigarettes a day so you're going to fucking die anyway. They should make a smoothie out of coffee and cigarette butts and call it "the rehab."

Several times a week they take us to an A.A. or N.A. meeting at night after dinner. N.A. is a place you can go without showering and look like everyone else there. We ride in a white van they call the "druggy buggy." These are the people I steered clear of when I went to meetings in the past, as if they had something contagious. Now I'm one of them. In case the druggy buggy wasn't shaming enough, it's obvious that we're from a rehab because none of us have any money to put in the basket, nor do we have phones. I sit next to Mackenzie in the van and stare at her lips for most of the ride, while she sings songs with the guys and cackles at her own jokes.

N.A. is way more hardcore and gritty than A.A. At the meeting a girl shared that she wanted to help her boyfriend get off heroin, so she went on it too so they could quit together. Good thing it was only heroin and not suicide. Fucking idiots. The ridiculousness and insanity of addiction was endless. A guy shared that he knew he had a problem when they started greeting him by name at the psych ward. He had been sober for twenty-one years and then relapsed. He said everything he learned was from Yale, Vail, or jail. I liked him.

After the meeting everyone stands outside and smokes. A black guy around sixty-five years old comes up to me and tells me I'm cute, then asks if I'm married. This is exactly why I don't get dressed up or wear makeup to meetings. I purposely look like shit, trying to avoid male attention. So that worked. I saw him inside the meeting and thought he was homeless, until he shared that he had money in his pocket. He tells me he's never been married and doesn't have kids. I congratulate him. He asks if he can give me his number, and I tell him I have three days sober and no phone.

When we get back to the town house we all sit around the campfire, except it's really just an overflowing ashtray with half-extinguished butts. We're all talking—me, Mackenzie, Ezra, and Justin—and I tell them that they're lucky to be here now while they're so young, that they have their whole lives ahead of them, and to stay sober so they don't ruin them. I warn them that they don't want to have to come back at my age after they're divorced, bankrupt, unemployable, and broken. I'm sure this is all falling on deaf ears, as most of them don't want to be there in the first place, have zero gratitude, and basically don't care. That's fine; if I were their age I would probably feel the same way. On a more optimistic note I saw a dog gate being carried in so I assumed the dog would soon follow.

DAY 6

Never check into rehab on a Friday or Saturday. Arriving on Friday is pointless because you do mostly nothing on Saturday. Arriving on Saturday is pointless because you do nothing Saturday or Sunday. Sundays are visiting day, which is pretty universal in most rehabs. We're allowed to have visitors from 1:00 p.m. to 4:00 p.m., and I was told that they don't search them or check their bags, so they can easily bring in drugs or weapons of mass destruction, which is essentially what drugs are.

On Saturday mornings we have yoga, except that day they didn't have any empty rooms for us to do it in so they made us do it outside, in the sun, while it's 85 degrees with 90 percent humidity. I tell Amanda I'm not participating, and she says if I don't I will get an assignment or lose phone privileges. I roll my eyes and sit in the shade alone. I feel like a five-year-old who has misbehaved. I can't believe I'm being threatened for refusing to contort my body in an outdoor oven. If this were junior high I would have had my dad write a note excusing me from class. I remember he wrote notes to get me out of swimming in the lake at sleepaway camp. Rehab is like psychological sleepaway camp, except there are no sports, you can smoke, and the counselors are called techs.

I watch the yoga class from under a tree and don't understand how any of them are doing it. It's so hot that I actually would go in the pool, if I hadn't cut off my nose to spite my face by not bringing a bathing suit. Jennifer is wearing jeans and sandals because she says her feet smell, and I'm literally losing my mind watching her destroy her yoga mat with them. Last time I was in rehab I barely did any exercise. They had a track behind the main facility, and I eventually got bored enough to start walking on it. I did around three laps and then saw a snake and never went outside again.

After yoga they take us to the beach, but it's optional. Since I live in Florida the beach is not exactly a treat, and I hate the sun anyway.

"Are you coming to the beach?" Amanda asks me.

"Do you have an umbrella?" I ask.

"No," she says.

"Then, no."

"OK, sunshine."

I can't stand her.

"Why don't they take us to a zoo or a museum?" I ask just to be annoying.

"Let me send an email."

That was the techs' response to everything. Can I call my mother? Let me send an email. Can my friend come visit on Sunday? Let me send an email. Can I jump off the terrace? Let me send an email.

And then it finally happened: the dog arrived. It's not a New-foundland as I had hoped, but a yellow lab named Ally. Besides the fact that Ally is a silly name for a dog, it's extra weird because there are already two Allys here. There's Ally, the heavyset girl from Maryland; Allison, who's black and a preacher's daugh-ter; and now Ally the dog. Ally is owned by Anna who's in the mood group. She tells us that Ally is a trained service dog, and we are not allowed to touch, distract, or make eye contact with her while she is working. She sits, perfectly quiet and obedient, under Anna's chair. She's so well behaved that she's almost boring. At night however, when Anna took Ally's work vest off, we were allowed to play with her, and quite frankly she seemed like a bit of a lunatic.

I remember the last time I was in rehab one of the counselors had a small, cute, white curly haired dog named Rocky. I went to visit him one afternoon in her office because I was bored, and she asked me if I wanted to walk him. Walk him? What was I, five? Why didn't they just give me the class hamster to take home for the weekend? How come I couldn't be trusted with a bottle of hair spray, or a razor, but I was trusted to walk her dog? And, by the way, in New York City people get paid $30 an hour to do that.

"Not right now," I said. I didn't want to do anything that involved taking care of him. That was my job at home. I really just wanted to take a nap with him, but didn't have the balls to ask.

A couple of days later I was desperate and bored enough to walk Rocky. We went past the gift shop, and I wondered if it would it be inappropriate to buy him a present. I had no other real friends there and wanted to do something nice for him. Unfortunately, all they had was recovery stuff. I walked him around the track a few times, but he couldn't focus. It was hot, and I was bored. When he started to hunt for snakes I returned him.

Saturday is movie night. The staff chooses the movie because if thirty addicts tried to agree on what movie to watch, just forget it. The last time I was in rehab they had pizza on Saturday nights and then forced us to play charades. It was supposed to be a sober "fun" activity. Sober, yes. Fun, no. I don't like movies so I went to make some phone calls.

I called Mindy. We spoke for a few minutes, and she told me some building gossip, how Coconut bit her ear, and that she missed me. I told her a funny story or two, and she said that I sounded different, clear. I suddenly realized that I'd never had a sober conversation with her. The entire time I'd known her I was high. Telling me I sound clear is pretty much the best compliment I can get right now. I never thought something as simple as that would boost my self-esteem so much.

DAY 7

Today I learned how blessed I am. I've somehow made it to rehab for the second time without having been arrested, molested, or received a DUI. I've never had an abortion, been divorced, or gotten tattoos I regret. How is this possible? Good thing close doesn't count.

A transgender person arrived today. Apparently they had a group meeting the night before to see if everyone was on board with this, but I didn't go because I wasn't feeling well. Anyway, her name is Nicole, she's twenty-four, and she's transitioning from a guy to a girl. She's super skinny with shoulder-length straight black hair, very pale skin, and red lipstick. She looks like Marilyn Manson. She's wearing a star of sorts around her neck, and I ask if she's Jewish. She says no, she's a witch and it's a pentagram. I'm getting an education worth millions here.

Nicole and I chat briefly, and she is quick to divulge that she OD'd on heroin and cocaine during a threesome, then she died, and then the paramedics brought her back to life and took her to the ER, wearing a lace top, boy shorts, and no shoes. I am completely intrigued by her, as she is clearly the most interesting person here—besides me and Miss I Wish I Were an Avocado. For some reason she and Mackenzie become instant best friends. I've literally never seen two people who don't know each other more than five minutes bond so quickly, like they were twins separated at birth. Dysfunctional drug addict twins.

Nicole shows up to group fully decked out. She's wearing a black skullcap that says #selfie, a black miniskirt, pink cropped t-shirt, and massive amounts of makeup and is clutching a stuffed Hello Kitty like it's her only hope. Did anyone frisk that Hello Kitty? She's also holding a hairbrush and continually brushes her hair, but it's more of a nervous habit than a grooming one. None of the women here get dressed up, and most don't wear makeup either, except for Melanie. Every morning when I see Melanie I'm always surprised by how put together she is and how much makeup she's wearing. It confuses me, and for a minute I always think she works here, or is going to a business meeting, or someplace important that the rest of us aren't allowed to go. I don't understand why she puts in the effort. I treated this "trip" like I would a vacation to Africa and brought minimal boring clothes and no makeup. The good thing about rehab is that it doesn't matter what you look like, as long as you're comfortable. You can eat, sleep, and go to group in the same clothes you slept in the night before and no one cares. Well, most people don't care. The last time I was in treatment I wore a tank top to dinner one night and one of the other patients told me that I was dressed inappropriately, and that I needed to cover up. I said I was hot. She said those were the rules. I told her to tell on me.

Nicole is sitting in her chair hunched over, sulking dramatically. She shares that she is very depressed and doesn't want to be here. She has a lot of shame and remorse, and says that she feels like "a piece of trash blowing in the wind." This is all delivered in the most deadpan, monotone, award-winning manner. It's just too good. I'm glad I unpacked.

We learn in group about process addictions. They're defined as any addiction besides drugs and alcohol—food, sex, gambling, shopping, etc.—and they don't address them here. So like, if you're also a sex addict that's nice, but it's your problem. Maybe in your spare time you can deal with that, but no one here wants to hear about it. Nicole isn't paying attention and turns to me and whispers: "I just need to get my eyebrows waxed and my nails done, and get more makeup."

They talk about social media being an addiction, which reminds me how much I don't miss that narcissistic bullshit. The counselor says that video games are a serious addiction and that people in China literally die because they sit there for hundreds of hours playing them and don't eat. Really? I'll have to fact check that when I get out. Anyway, I guess they don't go into detail about process addictions because it's all the same shit. We're powerless over everything: food, shopping, sex, other people, etc. Just fill in the blank and apply the same principles of recovery. A drug is a drug is a drug. I heard at a meeting once that saying you're an alcoholic and an addict is like saying you're from Los Angeles and California. I guess that sums it all up.

I have my second meeting with Stephanie. She asks me if I've ever written a letter to pot.

"Umm . . . no, but I've written letters to David Letterman and Donald Rumsfeld."

She suggests that I write one.

Dear Pot:

I hate you. It's because of you that I'm here. Well, it's because of me, I guess. But anyway, at first you were fun, you made me laugh and have a good time.

I thought you were my panacea, the medicine I needed,
my quintessential antidepressant. But you're insidious,
a wolf in sheep's clothing. After two years the laughing
turned to crying and the euphoria turned to lethargy
and self-loathing. You are a spiritual poison. Fuck off.

P.S. You owe me $8,000, plus the rehab fee.

Writing that letter is one thing, remembering it every single day of my life is another. This isn't high school, where you study for a test just to pass then forget everything you studied the second the test is over. This isn't something to take flippantly; this is my life. All I have to do every day is stay sober. That's it, that's my purpose. Stay sober and help another alcoholic, rather than get high and think about myself all day. It's not easy, but it's simple. I don't have to reinvent the wheel or write a best seller or make millions of dollars or save the world. And I especially don't have to compare myself to NASA. I'm worth more than my productivity. I'm good enough just being a sober person. I need to be grateful and appreciate what I have, instead of wanting what I don't have. Of course everything is a process. Awareness > acceptance > action. Plant > pet > relationship. Yale > Vail > jail. Jails > institutions > death.

That afternoon we have a drumming session. The drumming teacher is a heavyset, unattractive, middle-aged woman, with short frizzy hair and no makeup. Drummers are usually sexy and thin and men you might want to sleep with, but this is rehab in 2017, not a Mötley Crüe concert in 1990, and we got sage Broom-Hilda instead of drunk Tommy Lee. Anyway, drumming is pretty self-explanatory: you bang on different-sized drums for an hour to release pent up aggression or frustrations. Some of the drums are nice-looking and would make an interesting end

table, but besides that I find no solace in this. It's noisy and annoying, yet sadly the most exercise I've had in days. I tolerate it
for about five minutes, then I inform Broom-Hilda that I'm getting a headache, and she tells me to put my tongue on the roof of
my mouth, that it will help clear my thoughts. If this were a class
in high school, I would definitely cut next time.

I suddenly realize I haven't had an orgasm in a week.

DAY 8

And then it happened: I got a pimple. I walked over to the nurse's
station to get my pimple medicine, and the nurse told me she
would have to discuss it with the head nurse and that I should
come back in a little while. Huh?

I mean I get it. Everyone here is insane. All day long people
complain about headaches, stomachaches, nausea, any excuse to
get a pill. Every time I go to the nurse's station there's someone
trying to score some over-the-counter drug, moaning, "I have a
headache," or "I can't sleep," or "I have anxiety, cramps, pain, etc."
It's sad and boring, and the only thing they offer them is Tylenol,
which more or less does nothing for anything. It's basically the
same thing as melatonin or a lullaby.

But come on, I'm forty-seven years old. This is absurd. Being
in rehab is depressing enough, but being in rehab and breaking
out just adds insult to injury. Being in rehab and breaking out
and not being allowed to have your pimple medicine should be a
fucking crime. Did I need to call my attorney?

I told myself to calm down, that I don't run the place and
that maybe sometimes rules do apply to me as well. I know
there's a lesson in everything, even if the lesson was that these
people were hypervigilant, uncompassionate idiots. So I didn't

argue. I didn't threaten. I didn't raise my voice. I might have rolled my eyes a little, but it's progress, not perfection.

On the way back to my room I stopped at the techs' table in the courtyard. Tan Amanda was standing there pouring a half liter bottle of Coke Zero into a liter bottle. Someone told me she drinks seven of these a day. I'm surprised she's not dead. I say hi and she says "Not today!" Ugh. More like "Not funny."

We chat for a little, and she says, "You remind me of Daria." Isn't that like a ten-year-old cartoon character from the '90s? Whatever. I don't ask because I don't care. I notice the binder where people list the items they want from the drugstore. Twice a week the techs go to Walgreens for us. I'm curious to see what other people request, so when Amanda isn't looking I start thumbing through the pages. I mean if they don't want people to look through it they should put a lock on it, like the thermostat.

Person 1
Cigarettes
Coke

Person 2
1 lighter
12 pack Pepsi

Person 3
Cigarettes
Crest White Strips
Cookie dough
Lighter

Person 4
Stamps
Foster Grant sunglasses

Person 5
Diet Coke
Peanut M&M's (large bag)

Person 6
Lean Cuisine – 6 boxes

Person 7
Lighter

Cookie dough? Insane. Crest White Strips? Totally necessary in rehab. They should take everyone's cigarette and lighter money and donate it to cancer research and bring them back a note congratulating them on quitting. I'm sure that would not go over well, but at the very least it would be an interesting social experiment. Or a deadly massacre.

I walked back to the nurse's station. This time I went to a different window and the nurse gave me the medicine. What a victory. Well, a small victory for my skin but a large victory for my newfound patience and tolerance.

Every night in group they make us say our highs and lows for the day. This is painfully annoying, as everything seems like a low being stuck with a bunch of wackos in a semi-prison that's 14 degrees below zero. The only high I get is fantasizing about the sex I will hopefully have when I get out of this institute, but I can't share that so I make them up just like you make up feelings in the morning group. My high that day was having been granted the simple freedom of being able to tend to my basic needs. My low was having to work for it.

Rehab

DAY 9

There's an older woman named Diane in the mood group who doesn't speak. She's very pale with eyes popping out of her head, and she walks with a cane. She looks like a mental patient from central casting. Her hair is short and black and appears like she hasn't washed it in six months; you can literally see the oil and dandruff. She reminds me of Edward Scissorhands, minus the scissor hands. She scares me. If you say hello to her she doesn't respond. She never shares in the morning group, and I found out she hasn't left her house in two years, so I guess coming here is progress. I mean I've hardly left my house either, but I've had sex and I doubt she has, in decades.

Today we got a new girl in our house named Cassie, who will be Mackenzie's roommate. I'm introduced to her briefly, and then I go into the kitchen to get something to eat. I see a clear plastic container with Cassie's name on it on the counter. I open it up and there's a disposable razor inside. Since I haven't shaved in a week I quickly dry shave my legs in front of the refrigerator, then put the razor back in the container. I could have slit my wrists with that razor, and someone could have gotten fired for not locking it up, but I really just needed to shave, not die.

Cassie is this adorable tiny hippie doll from South Carolina. She maybe weighs a hundred pounds and has big green eyes, which she rolls in annoyance with alarming frequency. Her hair is brown and very short, and she wears it in little pigtails on the top of her head. She has the cutest southern accent and says words like "y'all," which would normally annoy me but she's an exception. She's the same size as me, has the same blood pressure as me, and eats like me. She's quick-witted, sharp-tongued, and won't take shit from anyone. I love her feisty rebellious character and her I-hate-everyone demeanor. She's as hard as nails.

She dropped out of high school. She spent a night in jail for destruction of property. She used to get high with her dad; she shot him up. She owns guns. She's twenty-four years old and has a two-year-old son and a soon-to-be-ex-husband. She only gained ten pounds when she was pregnant and claims her doctor said no one really needs to gain any more than that. Her drug of choice is heroin.

That afternoon we have acupuncture, which is one of the things I deemed a "waste of time" when I was originally looking over the schedule. I've never tried it before, but I decide to give it a whirl because I'll probably never do it outside of here, unless under some desperate circumstances. I mean more desperate than this.

Nicole refuses to partake and instead sits on the sidelines making inappropriate comments about all the guys' bodies. She says Justin has a great ass and that Al is a god. "Look at the shape of his body," she says too loudly. Later on Melanie gets her in trouble for this.

The acupuncturist looks at my tongue and says that I have anxiety and sleep problems. Neither is true but I don't say anything. This seems like a step above a magic wand. She puts a couple of needles in my back, and I sit there hoping to feel something. I won't let her put needles in my ears or on my face because I'm not *that* desperate. She moves on to Mackenzie after me. She asks to see her tongue and says, "Your tongue seems livery. Do you have anger?" I don't think anyone needs to look at her tongue to figure that out.

Twenty minutes later she takes the needles out of my back, and I don't feel any different. It kind of reminded me of meditation with Kiki, minus the banana and altar. At least I tried it and

I'm not high, so I can't confuse being stoned with anything this may or may not have accomplished.

DAY 10

I'd love to know what I was thinking when I decided to stay in Florida for rehab, for the second time. Oh wait, I wasn't thinking, I was high. Even though it's only April it's unusually hot, with intense humidity and mosquitoes everywhere. It's scorching outside and freezing inside, and I constantly go from one to the other because I'm just so uncomfortable in both places and it's driving me insane. This could really make a person want to get high, or jump off a third-floor terrace.

I'm worried about how Jackson is doing in his mini-prison. Is he homesick? Lonely? Is he wondering where I am? I'm sure if he knew he would be like "Thank god." There were times when I did stupid things when I was high and I swear he was looking at me like, "Go to rehab, bitch!" Now that I'm here I'm really disappointed that they don't have any kind of animal therapy besides a boring, too-well-trained dog that we're not allowed to touch 90 percent of the time. The ambitious side of me wants to open a rehab next door to this one. It will basically be the same, except there will be horses, sailing, personal chefs, and the temperature will never go below 72 degrees. We can just use the folders from this place, and they can get new ones that aren't misleading. The lazy, unmotivated side of me would rather complain about what this place doesn't have and live with the resentment.

Every few days some poor shattered soul shows up with a suitcase and the look of fear and despair. Occasionally someone shows up and seems totally fine, which was even more frightening. Today a new girl named Tiffany checked in. My mother wanted to name me Tiffany, but my father wouldn't let her. Instead I got named after a nonstick cooking spray. Anyway, Tiffany is only nineteen years old and has been to rehab five times already. She was stoned on methadone when she walked in. Did she forget to go to detox? I introduced myself to her and she told me I was pretty, then asked if I'd help her organize her closet. I said yes because I knew that in thirty seconds she wouldn't remember asking. A half hour later I heard Mackenzie introduce herself to her and Tiffany said, "You're so pretty." It reminded me of the time I took my dog to an old age home.

That night we went to an A.A. meeting nearby on the water. In the druggy buggy the guys all sit in the back and sing songs. It's kind of entertaining and funny.

"You guys should start a band," I said.

"Only if you're our manager," Al said. "We need someone like you—quick, dry, and a little bitchy."

I'm sitting next to Mackenzie and Nicole, and Nicole tells us that she can't wait to get a vagina and she can't wait to use it. Her dream is to carry a child. Mackenzie asks if she can design her own vagina. I'm shocked there isn't an app for that. Mackenzie starts saying how one of the techs is beautiful, and when she had to pee in a cup in front of her she was getting turned on. I know the tech she's talking about and she's very butch, which is disappointing, but not devastating.

At the meeting a guy in his late fifties shares that he was a microbiologist who blew up his home making meth. That's one way to become homeless. Another guy shared that if he drinks he's just gonna fuck up his life and end up in prison again, and then when they find out he's an addict they're gonna make him go to meetings, so rather than go through that whole cycle of insanity he'll just stay here. That's what they call playing the tape through. Impressive.

After the meeting we find Mackenzie outside screaming and waving her arms in the air like an out-of-control maniac. She got into a fight with someone who said that they'd rather be an addict than be mentally ill because it's easier to deal with. Mackenzie took this very personally and was so worked up I thought she was going to hurt someone. I've only seen this kind of anger and rage in movies. I thought she was going to have to be sedated, but then finally one of the techs calmed her down. More proof that she was not the kind of girl you should cross. Shutting off her TV when she wasn't looking was one thing, getting in a debate about addiction versus mental illness was another.

Later that night after the meeting Nicole is sitting at a table in the courtyard with Allison, the preacher's daughter from the south, who's in the mood group. They are talking about Satanism. Nicole says she is a Wiccan, a black witch, not a white one (whatever the fuck that means) and that she's been possessed by demons. She admits to casting spells on people. Allison is trying to spread God's word, while Nicole keeps saying she doesn't believe in god and that she controls her own destiny. Allison says she lives a contented life of joy and celibacy (even though she's engaged). She's not gonna have sex because ... well, I'm not sure why. Something about how sex is not happiness because happiness is fleeting. I ask her what she's here for and she says suicidal tendencies, depression, and trauma. It's not clear where the "contented life of joy" fits in, but whatever. Maybe if she had sex she wouldn't be suicidal or depressed. After twenty minutes I can no longer listen to this insanity. I want to go to my room and be alone, but then I will miss the camaraderie, excessive heat and humidity, and the secondhand smoke. To kill time I walked back and forth in the prison yard while sucking on coffee nips.

I come back twenty minutes later, and they're still talking.

A few hours after that Nicole confides in me that that entire conversation she had with Allison was all bullshit, that she was just bored, and admits she's a pathological liar. That's good to know; I'm glad I only listened to an hour of it. They say you're only as sick as your secrets, so I'm happy she confessed. I should probably confess about using Cassie's razor, but I don't think that makes me sick, I think it makes me practical.

DAY 11

A young guy named Cody checked in today. He's tall and skinny with thick black curly hair and big glasses. They introduce him to the group and ask him to tell us about himself.

"Hi, I'm Cody, and I'm from the Cayman Islands," he says.

"What brought you here?" the counselor asks.

"Well, my parents sent me because they were tired of me hanging around the house."

I can feel Cassie rolling her eyes.

"What's your drug of no choice?" the counselor asks.

"Huh?" He says.

"Your drug of choice."

"What's that?"

"This is a drug rehab."

"Oh shit. I just got invited yesterday."

Umm, is he in the wrong place? He's either the dumbest person alive or in more denial than anyone I've ever met. I'm leaning toward the former.

Rehab

Cassie confronts him: "I don't understand," she says with hostility. "Why are you here? Are you an addict? We're all addicts here."

It's the first time Cassie has spoken out in group, and I'm glad that our five-foot-two spokesperson is so passionate when it counts. Everyone is silent in anticipation of the answer to the 64-million-dollar question. Cody looks like a deer in the headlights. He wasn't expecting this kind of interrogation on his leave of absence from doing nothing. Eventually the counselor pries out of him that he does in fact smoke weed and that his parents think he has a problem, even though he thinks he doesn't. Either way he loves his parents so much that if they want him to be here he has no problem with it. It's like he's doing them a favor vacationing for a month in a rehab that no one else wants to be in for five minutes.

We move on from Cody and are given an assignment that says: "My ideal life looks like . . . ." We get about ten minutes to write our answers. I wish I could do this in Photoshop with pictures and maps, or via Snapchat filters with ears and a tail. I would have myself living on a goat farm in Beverly Hills, with a caretaker. There would be a dog farm next to the goat farm, with a caretaker. I would have the perfect fake tan, never age, and have sex with tons of hot guys at my discretion. I would eat sushi and caviar every day and write warped, irreverent books about being mentally ill in paradise.

I look around the room, and most people have written dozens of sentences, then I look over at Nicole's paper and it says, "I want to be a unicorn," with a smiley face. I'm dying.

We go around taking turns reading our answers out loud. Justin says he wants a certain type of engine for his car and wants to start a fight club. Ezra doesn't understand the assignment. "How do I know what I'm gonna want when I'm seventy-five?" he asks.

Nicole says, "I hope I'm dead."

The counselor tries to explain to Ezra that it's just how you see your life and try to imagine just the next three years or so. "How do I know where I wanna be in three years?" he asks. "I don't have twenty-twenty vision." Oy. I'm surprised he didn't give an answer like "I wanna win the lottery." If anyone here won the lottery they'd be broke or dead in a month.

After Nicole hears what other people wrote she looks down at her paper with remorse and says, "I didn't take this seriously at all." Then she whispers to me, "I just wanna be a housewife and be pampered. I want to look weak and dainty; I don't want any muscles. I want double D's and a big ass, and I wanna sit home in my fur coat petting my Chihuahua, and my husband will give me his credit card and fuck me."

"Don't write that," I said.

She rewrites hers, and we both realize we forgot to write "stay sober," so we shamefully squeeze it in at the top. Yikes.

During break Nicole pulls me aside saying she has to talk to me.

"What's up?" I ask.

"OK, so I have to tell you something. I'm attracted to Mackenzie."

"So am I," I said matter-of-factly. I mean I just thought everyone was.

She doesn't even acknowledge my response and continues: "I told her I was attracted to her, and she said that she thinks I'm pretty but she's not sure...."

"Maybe just give her time to process it," I said, although I knew that friendship was over.

That afternoon we have art therapy. The art teacher makes us throw a soccer ball around the room that has questions written all over it. No one knows what this has to do with art, but we just follow directions. Wherever your thumb lands is a question you have to read out loud. Mackenzie gets, "Do you like talking to strangers?" Turns out she loves talking to strangers because "There could be a guy in a clown suit who's going through the hardest time of his life." Nicole says she thinks strangers are going to kill her and that's why she carries a knife.

Someone lands on "What's the difference between sex and love?" and I said, "How would I know? It's been a long time since I experienced them both at the same time."

Next question: "If you could be a historical figure, who would it be?" Nicole says, "George Washington because he didn't smile, and I don't smile."

"He had wooden teeth," I said.

"I will eventually."

How this is supposed to help us stay sober is not exactly clear. I'm just going through the motions and trying to be "part of." I also can't imagine living without these people and this twenty-four-hour entertainment.

They pass around a coloring book, and we're supposed to pick a page and color it. I guess this is supposed to relax us or make us focus, but the lines we have to color in are so small that it gives me anxiety. The last time I colored I was able to see. Maybe that's why coloring books are designed for five-year-olds. The teacher puts on meditation music that's more creepy than soothing, and it makes me want to crawl out of my skin.

Melanie has her own coloring book that she has brought with her. That's normal for a woman approaching fifty. It's a cat coloring book, and she says when she's done with it she will give it to someone else who will find pleasure and joy from it. Does she think it's a fucking sex toy? No one wants your fucking cat coloring book. No one.

Next thing we know Nicole calls Ezra adorable and Ezra threatens to "pop" her if she says that again. Then he announces that he hates all gay people. Then Nicole calls him retarded. This escalates, and five hours later Ezra is under house arrest, which means he can't leave his townhouse for two days. He isn't allowed to do anything besides stand on the front porch. This gives him plenty of time to think about his behavior and smoke the three cartons of cigarettes his parents brought him on visiting day.

That night we go to an NA meeting in Delray Beach. There's a sign outside that says, "Weapons of any kind prohibited." Looking around as we wait to go in, it looks like a prison yard. It feels like if you make one false move you're gonna get shot or contract hep C.

"And I thought meetings in South Carolina were bad," Cassie says, looking around in fear.

"Just don't touch anyone," I warn. "That guy with the hat over there is kind of cute."

"Oh my god, Pam, seriously? You can do so much better."

"Oh."

"What do you do when a guy has a small dick?" Nicole asks.

"Leave," I said.

"Haaaa."

"I've been high for two years. I'm completely detached when I have sex," I said.

"I admire that about you," Cassie says.

"Does my makeup look OK?" Nicole asks.

"Yup."

"The other day I asked Melanie if my makeup looked OK,

and she said I could use some more blush. I just wanted her to say it looks OK. That's all I want anyone to say."

The night was a two-speaker meeting. The first guy shares a story about how he was out cheating on his girlfriend on Valentine's Day, and she kept calling him and he kept ignoring her until finally she left a message saying, "If you don't call me, I'm gonna hang myself." So he didn't call her, and she hanged herself. I was trying to figure out what the moral was there, if there even was one. Always call someone back? Don't date unstable lunatics? Don't cheat on unstable lunatics and not call them back, especially on Valentine's Day? All of the above?

The second speaker was a young woman who had been to hell and back—heroin and cocaine addict, sexually abused, hep C, cancer survivor, prison. The whole time she spoke I thought about Mackenzie. Apparently the whole time she spoke Mackenzie thought about herself too. After the meeting Mackenzie came up to me and said, "Holy shit that girl just told my story." She was going home in a few days, and we were all concerned about her. I encouraged her to ask for the speaker's number, which she did. We talked about the speaker in the van on the way back, and Mackenzie was so happy that she would have someone to connect with when she got out. When we got back to the rehab, I was the last one out of the van, and I looked down and saw the speaker's number on the floor. She couldn't even hang onto it for a half hour? That number was her lifeline. I picked it up to give it back to her, but I knew it wouldn't be long before it was lost for good. It made me sad. If she didn't go to meetings when she got out, she had no chance.

When I first moved to Florida I didn't go to A.A. meetings because . . . well, I had so many reasons. I didn't like this meeting because it was too cold. I didn't like that meeting because it was too dark and the people were gross. So I wound up getting high instead. Now I know that I don't have to like the meetings, but I still have to go to them. We go to meetings to not forget, to remember who we are and where we came from. Because it only takes two minutes of your life being good and you get ahead of yourself and then you're fucked. Or it takes two minutes of your life being bad and you think you can fix it again with drugs, which eventually leads you back to meetings. Or insanity. Or death.

Later that night there was big gossip in the courtyard. Mackenzie threw an apple core in the toilet, and Cassie was pissed because they share a bathroom, and the handyman didn't come until the morning. She rolled her eyes extra hard and long because she had to suffer the consequences of this act of complete idiocy, and I thought she was going to have a seizure. I called my mom and told her about art therapy, the apple core, and that I think I have lung cancer from living in an ashtray.

DAY 12

I have a dream that I'm making out with a guy and a girl at the same time. I write this down in my dream book although it's a secret. I'm only as sick as my secrets, dreams, and fantasies, although I can't tell one from the other. I haven't had an orgasm in thirteen days.

Today a woman named Dorothy checked in. She's fifty-nine and the oldest person here. Ironically she thinks I'm younger than the youngest person here thought I was. She thinks I'm twenty-six. I thought she was seventy-five.

One of the techs comes to the morning group with a special surprise for all the smokers. He brought these disposable things you breathe into, which checks your CO_2 level. For some reason everyone is excited about this. It's not a contest, it's a fucking health warning. Everyone's results were horrible and alarming, but nobody seemed fazed by them. No one mentioned quitting, but some vowed to "cut down." Everyone compared their results—and then went outside to smoke more. Fucking idiots.

We find out that Tiffany left. She didn't really need rehab anyway. Oy. Speaking of people who don't need rehab, it's Cody's turn to check in with the group.

"Tell us what's going on," the counselor says.

"Everything's going well," he says.

"How are you adjusting?" the counselor asks.

"Oh, I'm adjusted, thanks. I like the food." There's a long pause and silence in the room and then he says, "I'm just enjoying the rain and looking to get a glass of water and go outside and hang with people." He sounds like a special needs child.

Mackenzie is supposed to go home today, or transfer to an outpatient facility. She's been really nervous about it and crying on and off in group. She wasn't around all morning, and then when we were in our community meeting, we heard her in the room next door with one of the counselors, screaming at the top of her lungs. We couldn't understand what she was saying, but next thing we heard was that she ran off with only a cigarette and a Sprite. She left all her stuff behind, and after five hours, it was pretty clear that she wasn't coming back. We all knew the odds were that she was smoking crack on the streets. I go into her room and find her journal sitting on the nightstand. I figure since she left it here and isn't coming back, it's kind of fair game. She might not agree with that, but then again I'm sure she's not thinking about it. I open it and start reading. "This is the gayest place ever. Everyone here is lame." Even me? Or did she write that before I got here? Next page: "I really wanna stay sober but bitch I'm borrrrrreeeed." A few pages later: "I am truly blessed. This place is amazing." I will pray for her.

Now that Mackenzie is gone Nicole is moving into the town house with Cassie, Jennifer, and me. She didn't get along with the other girls in her house, specifically Melanie. She didn't like that Melanie told her to take her hair out of the sink. After her first few days of living there she came down one morning dressed very conservatively, more like a woman than a kid. I told her she looked nice and she said, "You like this? Melanie gave me some clothes. I'm Melanie now. I'm not gonna dress like a teenage slut anymore. And when a new girl comes I'm gonna act like Melanie and tell her to get her hair out of the sink."

Nicole's in her own room on the third floor. She has two huge suitcases and several bags, yet asks me for everything. Do I have face wash for acne? Toothpaste? A hair mask? I mean what is in those bags? Although she is technically still a guy, she asks one of the male techs to bring her bags upstairs for her and whispers to me, "I love having guys carry shit for me."

Later that day, around 5:00, I go outside to the courtyard, and everyone has made a group dinner that I wasn't aware of. The delicacies consisted of gumbo, pad thai, and rainbow cheesecake. Yuck. People here have such bizarre eating habits. Justin drinks Kool-Aid all day and brags about it. Allison, the preacher's daughter, only drinks smoothies. They're made of apples, sweet potatoes, and oatmeal, and every time I see her drinking one I want to throw up. At least half the women here only consume smoothies. Why don't people eat solid food anymore? Why must everything go in a blender? I know a lot of the girls here have eating disorders, but since we eat almost all meals in our town house, none of the staff knows if anyone is actually eating

Rehab

or not. The funny thing is that they all brag about being vegans or vegetarians, yet they drank and drugged almost to the point of death and now suddenly they're all health nuts.

We're sitting around eating, and Justin asks, "Pam, were you ever a cheerleader?"

"Are you serious?" I said. "I have no cheer."

A cheerleader? I mean I liked the outfits, and the pom-poms were cute, but when I found out you had to practice three hours a day after school and cheer in rain and snowstorms, I lost interest. Not to mention I was never exactly athletic. I mean I basically had a tutor for gym.

Someone says that a guy named Alex, who's an outpatient here, walked eleven miles for a job interview that day. They say you have to go to any length to stay sober, so I give him credit for that. It's funny when you think about the things you'll do to get high, but most people don't want to do anything to stay sober. I will stand outside with no jacket on in 32 degrees to get high but won't walk my dogs when it goes below 60 degrees. I had a friend who once cross-country skied up Park Avenue in a blizzard to get cocaine. So yeah, you do what you have to do. I can't say I'd walk eleven miles for an interview, but I'd definitely walk that far to get high. The walk back would be great.

It gets quiet for a minute, and then Ezra says, "I can't help thinking that we could have done something for Mackenzie."

"Something that seventeen other rehabs couldn't?" I ask.

We hear a helicopter overhead and wonder if it's looking for her. Her parents have called saying they haven't heard from her.

Everyone is making plans for when they leave here. The statistics are that only one out of two people will stay sober after treatment. They say if you look to your right and your left those people will probably relapse. Like, for example, when Anna leaves she's going on a cruise with her family where she plans on getting drunk. Jennifer says she will probably drink again, but it definitely won't be as bad as before. Ezra says he will most likely smoke pot and asks me if I think he can.

"You're in rehab for pot," I said. "No."

"Really?"

"Do you know the definition of insanity?" I asked.

"No. What's that?"

"Doing the same thing over and over again and expecting different results."

"Wow," he says.

I can't believe these people are talking about drinking and getting high. Guess they forgot how they got here. Luckily, I haven't. I wouldn't want to go back to that stoner "life" for a second. Laugh till you cry, smoke till you choke, eat till you wanna puke. Get fat, get stupid, get emotional, lose your sanity, and then blame it on everything else. If someone ever "did to me" what I did to myself I'd sue them for monetary damage, time lost, pain and suffering, and emotional distress. But not everyone was planning their relapse. Nicole's goal was to get laser hair removal and buy herself gold teeth, and Cassie wants a tattoo of a palm tree abducted by an alien. Everyone else will probably file for bankruptcy and/or get divorced. All I wanted was to never again feel as awful as I did when I got here.

Then something bad happened. Cindy, one of the girls in the mood group, broke the rules and tried to jump off her terrace. If I were going to kill myself I would have definitely done it before rehab. Oh wait, that's what we were all trying to do. Now we're trying to save ourselves, I forgot. Anyway, I'm assuming this has been attempted before, and if they don't want it to happen again, why don't they just lock the terrace doors? I'll ask one of the techs who will tell me she'll send an email. Another issue is that when Cindy comes back from the psych ward she'll probably need a new roommate because her roommate was Annabelle whose father committed suicide, and that's just a tad too close to home.

That night we're in the druggy buggy on the way to an N.A. meeting when the driver who's one of the techs says, "Where's Franky?" I freak out. He means Franky, the lesbian from Wentworth. He means Mackenzie. No one else but me seems to get this. I like that.

We're all talking, and I tell Cassie that although she's smaller than me, she's way tougher. Then Jessica, who's from the mood group and calls me "Pammy from Miami," says, "You're pretty tough. The mood girls were scared of you when you first got here."

"Really?" I said. "Why?"

"You're from New York. You were like, 'I don't fucking say good morning.'"

"Ha ha. I was a misery when I got here. But Cassie shoots an AR17."

Cassie rolls her eyes.

"Do you eye roll during sex?" I ask. "I have."

"Yeah, when they can't complete their task par to my expectations I am eye rolling the entire time. And then I tell them to get the fuck off before I vomit on them."

"That's sweet of you to give them a warning."

Then a fire engine goes by with the siren on and Jessica starts to shake and cry. She was in a car accident six months ago, and her husband flew through the windshield and died right in front of her, that's why she was in treatment. When I first heard her story I asked if she was hurt and she lifted up her shirt revealing an eighteen-inch scar going down the center of her chest. I feel so bad and try to console her, but she seems to have learned how to calm herself down, and within a minute of taking deep breaths she seems to be OK. So sad, but I'm happy to see that the treatment is actually helping her cope better. There's hope for all of us.

DAY 13

The last time I was in rehab I left AMA. I left only three days early, but they were not happy about it. I remember vividly that when I told the staff I was leaving they called me into an office and tried to scare me into staying longer. They warned me that it was in my best interest to stay, and that if I left I wouldn't stay sober, would never get better, would probably die, etc. I knew that was protocol and that they were a business trying to make money. (Jennifer told me she overheard one of the therapists saying to another: "High five. I just got them to stay another week!") I assured them that I was so miserable there that that alone would certainly keep me sober, in order to prevent myself from ever having to go back. I would go to any lengths to never be institutionalized again. They told me that when I left I needed to adhere to a strict aftercare program. I needed A.A., M.A., S.A., Al-Anon, and ACoA. I needed one-on-one therapy, group therapy, and medication for depression. If I had any time left after that, I should exercise and get a job. If I didn't already have dogs I probably would have had to get one or two, or possibly even a horse. I basically needed to drop out of life in order to have time to deal with all my addictions. There was a lot wrong with me and not much hope. And they wondered why I was depressed. But like I said I stayed sober for eight years after checking out of that place, and to this day,

I don't regret leaving early. I really don't think three days would have made a difference in anyone's recovery, and using scare tactics just isn't nice.

For my last homework assignment I was forced to make a timeline of my life. It's twelve feet long and not funny. It was a lot of work and should probably have been a punishment rather than a requirement for graduation. It's like a final for rehab. I was ready for my diploma.

I'm leaving tomorrow and was called into one of the offices to speak to the guy responsible for discharge. His name is Jorge, and he's been working here for about five minutes. He has my phone in his hand and before he gives it to me he asks if I deleted my dealer's phone number? I said no.

He hands me my phone. It's like a precious piece of jewelry I haven't seen in a while. It looks so crisp and clean, and I'm so excited to have it back in my hands. The only problem is it's dead. He takes it back and plugs it in, and I sit there with massive anxiety waiting for it to charge. What will be on it? Who texted me? I mean most people know where I am but you just never know. I want to look up Mackenzie. I'm scared that if I go on Facebook I'll find out she's dead.

The phone finally starts up and I have 33 texts, 15 missed calls, and 217 emails, and that doesn't include the other missed calls and tons of texts I never responded to before I got to rehab. Is it wrong to say to someone, "Sorry, but I've been too high to follow up with you for the past two years?" Because I need to send that message to about twenty people.

The first thing I do is find Lucky's number and delete it. Then I look at my texts. The most recent text is from an idiot ex-boyfriend. He sent a picture of his stupid dog in front of a winery and writes, "How's sober life?" The problem with going to rehab is that the rest of the world doesn't change. You work on yourself all day long for weeks and you come out and everyone is still an asshole. You think so much has gone on while you've been in there but really not a single thing has changed—except hopefully you.

I quickly glance at my emails, which I assume are mostly junk. I open the most recent one:

info@ ██████████████   3:59 PM ⬤
To: Home Jo
Re: Jackson Gaslow

Hi Pam,
Jackson did well on his first day, roamed around and mostly kept to himself, following the handlers a lot and getting lots of attention from them. He didn't feel up to eating breakfast his first morning with us but seemed to have no problem with his appettie the rest of his vist. He was in and out of the pool and did do a bit of napping. He also has a slightly bad habit of mounting other dogs and getting snappy if they get too close to his nap area but he seemed to enjoy himself and the pool and found a new best friend (named Harry) to pal around with.

Feel free to contact us with any other questions and we look forward to seeing you guys again in the future.

██████████████████
██████████████████

The rest was garbage. The weird thing is that there were basically no charges on my credit card for the past two weeks. I should check out of life more often. This is the longest trip I've ever been on where I didn't buy anything.

I hand the phone back to Jorge. "Can you remove the handcuffs now?" I joke. He doesn't get it.

Jorge makes me fill out some forms listing ways I will work on staying sober and three hobbies I will develop. Isn't this where I started, thinking hobbies would save me? I write down "learn chess" and "take Spanish lessons." I'm sure I will do neither, but I don't care. I've never heard a recovery story where someone was saved by their hobbies. Besides, I feel strong and motivated. Not to learn Spanish, but to live.

"How come no one's asked me to stay longer?" I asked. I was curious why I wasn't being bombarded with pressure. Almost insulted actually. Didn't they care about me?

He looks at me and says. "You're more than welcome to stay!"

"Yeah, no thanks."

I mean you gotta deal with the real world again eventually. And the good news is I still have my job when I leave: cleaning up after two dogs. But seriously, I feel healthy and confident, like someone capable of handling their own cell phone, razor, and hair spray—plus whatever nonsense may randomly show up on my phone from people I now call "Idiots of the Past." Then again there's also that wonderful blocking feature.

Later that night Cassie, Nicole, and I are hanging out in the kitchen of our town house. Cassie is eating peanut butter out of the jar and cut-up apples with honey. She's been scribbling in her journal all night and asks me if I want to read it. I say of course.

"Rehab is hell. Everyone's 'afraid' to go home. Fucking pussies. I'd trade places with them in a heartbeat." On Mackenzie: "She was an invalid who reminded me of Angelina Jolie's character in 'Girl Interrupted,' but less bold, and diagnosed with Tourette's. Her laugh made my soul leave my body."

"You're funny," I tell Cassie. Oddly I feel uncomfortable reading anymore although she offered it to me and not vice versa.

"It's your last night, we should do something fun," Nicole said.

"Umm, like what?" I ask.

"I don't know."

Cassie is now standing on a chair looking through the top cabinets for food. I'm starting to think something is wrong with her. She gets down, walks out of the room, then comes back and asks me if I have rubber gloves.

"Huh? For what?" I said, as if I actually had them but needed to know what she was going to use them for before I gave them to her.

"I want to clean the sink in the laundry room," she says.

"Why would I have rubber gloves?" I ask.

"I don't know, because you're a sex addict."

"Right. And you're a lunatic."

Help another alcoholic. Except if they ask you for rubber gloves. Then just pray for them.

"Funny because I didn't bring rubber gloves," I said. "I also didn't bring a teddy bear, a vibrator, or a gun. I followed all the rules, and now I'm ready to get the hell out of here. But I do love you, my friend."

DAY 14

In A.A. they say don't give up five minutes before the miracle. Well, today a miracle happened. Diane, the mute woman, spoke in the morning group for the first time ever. She didn't say much, but she said her name and that she was going to try to be more present. It literally felt like a scene out of a movie and everyone in the audience had their mouth agape. The whole room clapped extra loud and yelled "Good morning!" And she sort of smiled. It was more like a Wednesday Addams–type of smile, but speaking and smiling is a lot for one day. For half my life strangers used to tell me to smile when they walked past me in the street, and I hated it. I was like, who are you to tell me what to do with my mouth? How do you know my cat didn't just die? Or I missed getting laid by a matter of seconds? Or that I simply couldn't. My point is that I kind of understood Diane. She did the best she could, and her progress inspired all of us.

On your last day in treatment they give you a "Rock Star" ceremony. They pass around some sort of stone in the shape of a star, and everyone says something nice about you or wishes you luck or whatever. It's awkward since some of the people have only been here a day or so and have no idea what to say. People offer the generic "I've seen you come so far," and "wish you the best," etc. When it's Cody's turn he says, "I don't really know what to say except that you're dope, and I like your glasses." Oy. Finally it's Cassie's turn and she cries and then I cry. I'm really gonna miss these guys; they feel like my second family. Or maybe my first. Except for Cody.

I go to collect my meds and they pull up my file on the computer. I see a picture of myself the day I checked in: my rehab mug shot. I look sad and stoned, a lost soul with dead eyes. It's so upsetting to see a photo like that of yourself and to know that it's not even yours to delete. All I can do is thank God I no longer feel how that person looks. Thank God I'm not that dead person anymore.

I was standing outside waiting for my mother to pick me up and realized I needed to say one final goodbye.

Dear Pot:

The more time we have away from each other the more clarity I get. This was the longest most pernicious relationship I've ever had, and you were never gonna be the one to end it. You were going to take me further

down the abyss of hopelessness and despair, putting
a permanent pause button on my life. Seeing what I
looked like under your spell is tragic and terrifying,
and also the best reminder of all the harm you caused,
of everything you took away from me. You brought out
the worst in me and thank God I had the strength and
courage to end that before it was too late. You have
nothing I want.
I want to be present. I want to feel. I want to be free.
I want self-respect. I want to face my fears one day at
a time, because no matter how scary they are, you're
way scarier. But most of all I want to live, and you're
the opposite of life. You're a soul sucker, a mind fuck, an
insidious all-encompassing toxicity. You're a destroyer
of spirits, love, hope, dreams, ambition, productivity,
time, memory, lungs, and brain cells. I don't remember
a lot about the last two years, but at the same time I
remember too much. Adios.

They say the goal in recovery is to be happy, joyous, and free. I'm not a happy or joyful person by nature, and I never have been. I don't wake up in the morning eager to seize the day. I joke that I'm missing the gene that enables you to get excited, except it's the truth. I've been to therapists on and off since I was fifteen and I'm on antidepressants and I understand that for the most part I will always be this way. It is unlikely that I will have a personality change at forty-seven, or ever. I work daily at accepting that this is my life and not beating myself up because I'm not joyous like other people. There are things that help and others that don't. It's all trial and error and figuring out what's right for you. Magic wands are insulting. People telling me to smile is ineffective and rude. A.A. meetings are my medicine. Exercise and something satisfying that fills my time are also critical. As long as I try my best to embrace my imperfections and attempt to help another person, that's all I need to do. As long as I'm not self-medicating, I'm a winner. As long as I'm not putting a depressant into my body 24/7 thinking it's going to cure my depression, I have a shot. Life has ups and downs and some days I'm "happier" than others. But I try to appreciate the good things I have and not take them for granted. There's a line that Carrie Fisher wrote in *Postcards from the Edge*: "She had plenty of evidence that she had a good life. She just couldn't feel the life she saw she had. It was as though she had cancer of the perspective." I've learned that the opposite of misery and fear is gratitude. I might not have everything I want but I can eat, breathe, walk, etc. I know every day is going to be a challenge, and I have no expectations. I'm just happy to be sober and not a zombie prisoner of my own mind. If I stay clean the possibilities are endless. If I get high there are none. Someone recently asked one of my friends, "Is Pam happy?" He was like, "Happy? She has a blog called *Depressed Hot Girl*." I laughed because it was perfectly stated. And right now, this minute, I am happy. Because I'm free. And when my mom gets here I'm going to get in the driver's seat and drive myself to a drugstore or a supermarket and shop on my own without supervision. I'm gonna buy whatever the fuck I want to, because I can. I'm gonna pick up my crazy untrained con artist dogs, bring them back to my apartment, and let them run amok. I'm gonna check out my ass in the full-length mirror, to make sure it hasn't changed. If it passes the test, I will then reunite with my estranged vibrator and finally have a fucking orgasm.

Pam Gaslow is a New York–born, Miami-based writer, comedian, and artist. She's a contributor to *The Huffington Post*, *The Good Men Project*, *The Times of Israel*, and *Newsbreak*. Pam used to have a blog called Depressed Hot Girl, but she took that down after her family threatened to disown her. For more salacious details and quirky randomness, follow her on **Instagram @pamgaslow.**